Edited by

AHMED ADETOLA-KAZEEM

THRIVE

A compendium of teachings on resilience and growth strategies for a successful career and business.

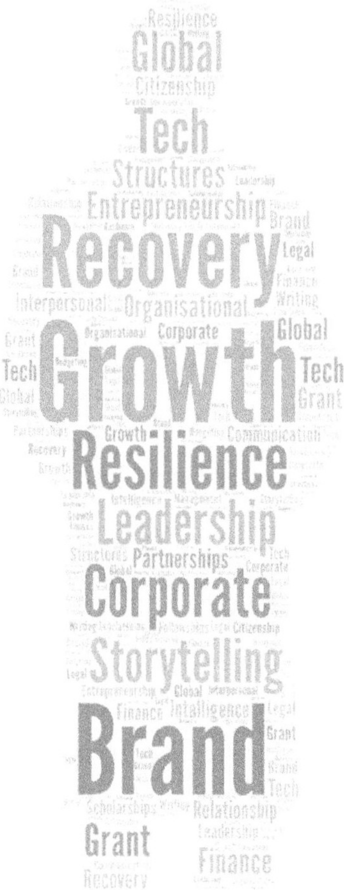

THRIVE

A compendium of teachings on resilience and growth strategies for a successful career and business.

Layout: Austin Aiyedatiwa
Cover Design: Ahmed Shoyombo
Printed and Bound at Thrifty Hands Enterprise, Lagos.

Published by
Thrifty Hands Enterprise
Tel: +234 803 500 6512
nigeriathrifty@gmail.com

# DEDICATION

This is for my late dad----mentor, inspirer and boss

CONTENTS

FOREWORD

One obvious fact in this world is that when one person thrives, many people around him/her thrive too. It starts with someone – who by improving himself/herself and caring after his/her well-being can create a positive ripple effect not only in his/her life but in the lives of those around him/her. So, everybody needs to keep thriving.

I am the founder, Chief Executive Officer and chief ideas evangelist of SB Telecoms & Devices Limited, a proudly Nigerian award-winning ICT company that developed TAMS, a time management focused web-based biometrics and human resources management solution. I also double as the CEO of ZKTeco Biometric Limited which was recently incorporated in Nigeria.

I am privileged to be acquainted with Ahmed through my younger brother Kazeem Abiodun, who was his school mate. Our path crossed fully during his short stint with us at SB Telecoms and Devices Limited and during this short but remarkable stay, he was able to exhibit his selflessness, dedication, commitment, result oriented mindset and versatility. His desire to succeed is second to none as I remember vividly how resolute and resilient he was to get results for his team.

Since that experience while he was at SB Telecoms, he has never looked back as I have equally been following his steady rise to prominence and relevance through sheer determination, diligence and resilience. I have marvelled at the way and manner he has been able to create time for everything he is doing and still able to excel in all of them. He is a good manager of time and resources which is what is required to be a good leader. As the Nigeria time keeper, myself. I know what it takes to keep to time without defaulting.

As a focused, energetic and ambitious person who has worked diligently to create a niche for himself as a motivator, mentor, champion and a role model for others, I can confidently say that he is more than qualified to come out with a book about thriving. I have known him to be a forthright and dogged fighter who leaves no stone unturned to achieve success in whatever he sets his mind to do. He is indeed a true goal getter to the core.

I am not surprised that a book of this nature is coming from him despite his youthful age - he has achieved more than his age. He has passed through all the stages covered in this book. As a mentor who has also gone through mentoring himself, he was able to highlight the types of mentorship in existence and the benefits accruable to both the mentee and the mentor. He further advises people to feel free to seek mentoring to make a lee way while also listing out some of the advantages that are available to those who accept to be mentored.

The book is a compilation of wealth of experience of young professionals from different backgrounds, careers and works of life. The Editor due to his experience, expertise and versatility carefully selected these persons as facilitators at the AAK Mentorship Programme and their presentations is what has been compiled into a book.

The book x-rayed the act of purposeful storytelling especially in applications and its positive effects when applying it to one's business. The book further highlights the strategies of writing applications to win scholarship and fellowship as well as the benefits of winning a scholarship or fellowship from a practical perspective. It also demonstrated how some of the questions asked while applying for scholarship or fellowship are answered.

One of the chapters in the book elucidates on building business for financial growth, erecting organizational structures and fostering partnerships. There was also a chapter on how to cope with setbacks and effectively overcome them while giving hints on how to run a profitable social enterprise. Legal tit-bits that will be of immense benefit for business start-ups was equally shared.

Advancement and opportunities in the global space with emphasis on the need to acquire new skills in the tech world as well as maximizing the opportunities that are inherent in the information and communication technology space to achieve more in this COVID-19 pandemic period was comprehensively dealt with.

The need for corporate leaders was clearly established in this book as it relates to challenges that are associated with becoming a great leader and how to tackle them while also highlighting the qualities that are expected of a good leader. It is quite ironical that one of the major problems bedevilling Nigeria is dearth of selfless and quality leaders. I hereby recommend this book for those aspiring to be at the helms of affairs to learn a lot from it.

I need to reiterate here that as a mentor, serial entrepreneur, business owner, corporate leader of repute and a major stakeholder/player in the ICT world, I am highly honoured and elated to write the foreword to this book because I have walked the talk and by virtue of my experience, exposure, education and expertise, I can confidently tell you that the contributors have done justice to the subject matter. This book is worth reading for everybody who aspires to reach the pinnacle of his/her business, career or academic pursuit. It is also recommended for those who are striving to find their feet in their different endeavours. The book has covered a wide range of human endeavours and therefore will be a good companion for everyone across diverse occupational pursuits.

Everybody will have something to benefit from it based on its focus areas because we all want to succeed and to succeed in life require continuous re-evaluation of our strategies and processes which is what THRIVE has come to offer.

The editor has done extensive work in researching, collating and compiling his facts which are obvious in the way and manner the points are articulated and presented in the book. The guidelines and the strategies discussed are well thought out and very practicable without ambiguity.

It is pertinent for us to note that what Ahmed has come to show us through this book is that "The way to thrive is to help others thrive; the way to flourish is to help others flourish; the way to fulfill oneself is to spend oneself" as stated by Cornelius Plantinga. We all need to continue thriving and one way to achieve that is by getting a copy of this book.

AFOLABI ABIODUN
CEO, ZKTeco West Africa

ACKNOWLEDGEMENTS

I am grateful to Allah for making this book come to reality. Without Him we are nothing. My appreciation goes to my parents for instilling in me the values of selflessness, contentment and integrity. I thank my siblings and my extended family under the leadership of Mr. Hassan Olufunso Yusuf, for being pillars of support at the very trying times when we lost our dad and our world seemed to fall apart.

Olatunji Adegbite paid a huge role in giving insights on how well to run the mentorship programme where materials for the publication of this book was gathered. He also contributed a chapter in the book.

I appreciate all the contributors to this book namely, Mr. Disu Kamor, the Executive Director of Muslim Public Awareness Centre (MPAC); Onyedikachi Ekwerike; Usman Ali (Farmer in Suit); Kabiru Olanrewaju; Kehinde Oseni; Hammed Kayode Alabi (Kayfactor); Abisola Akinrin; Fuad Shobowale; and Nojeem Subomi Yusuf. Most of them played additional roles of editing and proofreading, they also gave meaningful suggestions that greatly improved the quality of the book.

I must single out the industry of Yusuf Shin-Aba, Ruhamah Ifere and Akinola Akinsola who transcribed all the presentations and assisted in the editing and the general coordination of the mentorship programme. I appreciate my sister Karamah Shogbuyi, Enitan Oluwa, Hafiz Akinde and Olatunde Ojerinde for proof reading the transcribed texts and suggesting improvements.

Ahmed Shoyombo was the phenomenal designer of the cover of the book- he blew our minds with his simple but classy design. I appreciate the unassuming Tola Oni who graciously printed the book.

I express my profound gratitude to Mr. Afolabi Abiodun, CEO ZKteco West Africa, for writing the book's foreword. He has always been a pillar of support.

I appreciate all Mentors and Mentees of the AAK Mentorship Programme for their instrumental roles in making this book come into fruition.

Special thanks to my wife, for her moral support and for taking care of the home while I kept late nights ensuring that this book becomes a monumental success. I appreciate all staff of Adetola-Kazeem Legal Practice (AKLP); all volunteers of Prisoners' Rights Advocacy Initiative (PRAI); and all athletes of Q-MADI Taekwondo Club who have been a huge part of my journey.

I thank the Mandela Washington Alumni Fellowship Association of Nigeria (MWFAAN); FEGO Millenium Class; OOU Class of 2007; OOU Muslim Alumni; SB Telecoms & Devices Ltd; and LEMU Welfare Committee, your support for me over the years have been phenomenal and I do not take it for granted.

To all supporters of my work - known and unknown- I appreciate you all and pray that Allah reward you all abundantly.

Ahmed Adetola-Kazeem
August 2020

INTRODUCTION

During the lockdown, the world came to a halt. In the loneliness and boredom, I ruminated on some mistakes I had made in the past and opportunities I missed because I lacked some skills and mentors in specific areas. I felt I owed others the duty to guide them in order to avoid the pitfalls I had encountered.

I conceptualized the AAK Mentorship Programme where participants were attached to accomplished mentors. On a weekly basis, participants were treated to talks on career, business and personal development strategies. The topics covered storytelling; leadership; social intelligence; brand communication and management; global citizenship; climbing the corporate ladder; overcoming setbacks; running profitable social enterprise; opportunities in tech; benefits of being mentored etc.

The weekly presentations have now been compiled into a book for the benefit of those who did not attend and might not be able to attend future mentorship programmes. It will also be a good reference material for those who attended the mentorship programme or will attend in future.

Are you looking for a book to serve as a training manual for corporate staff, social entrepreneurs, tech enthusiasts, management staff or soft skills development generally? Are you a youth struggling with finding your career path? Wondering what is the next stage in accessing opportunities to fulfill your dreams? Confused about managing a profitable business yet making social impact? Or totally clueless about dealing with people and dealing with potential connections?

What if you can get answers to all your questions from one source, a book that identifies your problems and proffer intellectual and practical solutions, highlighting the step by step approach to a successful career and business, with emphasis on the core values of resilience, recovery and growth.

Ahmed Adetola-Kazeem

MENTORSHIP

GAINS OF MENTORSHIP

A COMPILATION OF THE MENTORSHIP JOURNEYS OF OUTSTANDING MILLENNIALS

AHMED ADETOLA-KAZEEM

During the early days of the lockdown, I had a deep reflection on how I have had to struggle to achieve a lot of things due to a lack of mentors. Even more depressing is how it has been difficult to achieve a lot of other things those who had mentors achieved easily. Upon deep reflection, I felt there was a need to share my story so that others could learn from my mistakes and soar above their pairs. In preparation for the experience sharing zoom session, I interviewed some outstanding individuals who are mostly millennials about how mentorship contributed to their successes. Their stories really inspired the audience and their feedback birthed the AAK Mentorship Program.

The beautiful stories of these inspirational personalities are shared below, I hope it inspires you to take mentorship seriously.

INFORMAL MENTORSHIP

NOJEEM SUBOMI YUSUF (Manager, Deloitte)

Mentorship has been helpful in a way, though I think it didn't come as early as I would have loved it. But for predestination, maybe if I was exposed to the quality of informal mentorship I started getting a few years back, I may have had a more rapid career growth.

So, when I didn't have mentors, I was living every day as it passed by; and in that time, my career growth was just by grace (and maybe innate intelligence), not because I was doing anything special.

Now, mentorship has helped me to identify my ultimate career goals and how I should ensure my daily activities are targeted towards achieving that ultimate goal. So, mentorship has helped me to be a lot more focused, to major in only the things that matter and not just doing everything that comes my way.

Before now I was almost always interested in every job opportunity that was going to pay good money, but now I look beyond the short-term benefits and properly assess every opportunity before I attempt to go for it.

One of the fruits of that mentorship is getting to Deloitte. I was clear I needed to get back to a Big 4 to attain African wide thought leadership in tax, which appears to be the ultimate (goal) for me. But then, because I was out of consulting for a while; no Big 4 was willing to give me a level that I thought was good enough. My mentors then mentioned to me to begin to show thought leadership even in my small capacity; this is the reason I started writing about tax on LinkedIn. Ultimately somebody in Deloitte was actually following me and then invited me for a conversation. The rest they say is history.

Deloitte is only a path to the top, it's not likely to be the top itself."

CHOOSE A MENTOR THAT ALIGNS WITH YOUR PHILOSOPHY

FARUQ ABASS (Lawyer, Arbitrator and Politician)

Mentoring has assisted me greatly in my career as a commercial litigator because I was exposed to the rudiments of the practice of law from my first year at the bar till date. I learned so much from working directly with Mr Candide-Johnson, SAN and most of what I learned from him are what I have adopted in running my firm—my style of preparing for a lawsuit, research, drafting, preparation of legal opinions, interacting with clients and general conduct at the bar were learned from my working relationship with Mr Candide-Johnson, SAN. It is instructive to state that I met Mr Candide-Johnson (SAN) at a young lawyers conference, which I attended in 2010 and I made up my mind that I was going to work with him because he appeared to me as a disciplined, eloquent and forthright legal practitioner when he addressed us at the seminar.

I also consult regularly with Mr Mutiu Ganiyu, the Managing Partner of Smithworth Partners, who has been my mentor for over 7 years and I usually learn a new principle of law, unique precedent or a recent authority whenever I interact with him—he is that good! I have also tried to emulate his strong research skills and my regular association with him keeps me on my toes on the need to keep improving my knowledge on a daily basis.

Another thing I learned from him is the habit of investing in good books. It is instructive to state that I met Mr Mutiu Ganiyu by sheer happenstance when I visited my friend who used to work for him and I was enamoured by his deep knowledge of the law and litigation process during my brief discussion with him (less than 10 minutes)—he recognized my name from a Reply Brief of Argument, which I drafted at the Court of Appeal when my friend introduced me to him!! I did not hesitate in adopting him as my mentor about 8 years ago—I don't regret this decision. I have certainly been blessed beyond measure by my regular interactions with him and I will not trade this relationship for anything. Thankfully, I live just about 4 blocks away from his residence.

Most importantly, I learned my solid work ethic from my parents—who were my first mentors, as I grew up observing them working very hard, reading regularly and upholding integrity as one of their core values. As an employee with Aboyade & Co. during my NYSC in 2010, an employee with Strachan Partners from 2010 till 2014 and an employee with Aelex Law Firm in 2014, I never got late to Court on any occasion and I was usually one of the first lawyers to resume at the office during my days in paid employment—I learned this from my parents.

In sum, I am not sure I would have been the same person that I am today if the Almighty God did not give me the privilege of learning directly from my parents, Mr Candide-Johnson, SAN and from Mr Mutiu Ganiyu on a regular basis. I also have other mentors for various other parts of my life (e.g. business, politics, family, social skills, religion and so on), but I have decided to limit this piece to my mentors in the legal profession.

GETTING MENTORED AND MENTORING OTHERS TO WIDEN YOUR SPHERE OF INFLUENCE

ABAYOMI OKUBOTE (Founder, Association of Young Arbitrators)

I have not always had a formal mentor although informally, people had at one time or the other mentored me. Whilst we did not sit down to agree to a mentorship plan, my line partner at Olaniwun Ajayi had invested in me by taking his time to teach me many things that I know now - which has shaped some of the things I do. The lesson in this is that you may have a mentor and may not necessarily know.

I had a formal mentor for the first time in 2017 when I organized the mentorship programme for Young Arbitration Practitioners in Africa. I also participated in the initiative and was mentored by a partner in one of the top international law firms in London. This was more formal.

At the beginning of the mentorship, we had a plan and milestones were set. It was indeed a rewarding experience as my mentor would take time to speak with me for hours and gave useful career advice. He also showed Interest in my initiatives and through him, I met many people in his firm. The lesson from this is that whilst this was only for six (6) months, it was as useful as the informal one with my partner because targets were set and we tried to achieve them. Again, when I started my PhD programme, my lecturer became my mentor and till date, he is the best mentor I have had. He did not only take interest in my PhD project; he also took an interest in my initiatives and was always there to give constructive but very useful feedback/advice. The mentorship still continues since I haven't finished my PhD programme and I can't wish for more.

I have tried to give back myself and I have several people I also mentor. I have learnt a lot from mentoring people - new ideas, developed new relationships, and made new friends. The truth is, the success of many things that I do today, is based on people's confidence, which the new friendship I gained from mentees has helped with. Mentees are everywhere speaking good of you and your name has travelled to places you haven't been to physically. Mentoring people has challenged me a lot and given me a different world view of how people perceive things.

BE BOLD TO ASK FOR MENTORSHIP AND MAKE THE MOST OF YOUR RELATIONSHIP WITH YOUR MENTOR

SEGUN FATUDIMU (Founder, Sozo Leadership Institute)

I have always had a different or, maybe, broader definition of mentorship. Mentorship to me is not only the conventional vertical relationship but can also be horizontal as well. This understanding of Mentorship makes me have different categories of mentors. Mentors are 'people' with significant levels of experience and expertise in areas of life and career that I admire. I have mentors that are peers and mentors that are very much older and advanced than me. These mentors have played significant roles in my personal and professional life. For the sake of this writing, I will share insights from my relationship with the more advanced/older mentors. Here are 5 key insights that I can think of:

1. Do not be shy to ask for mentorship - One of my mentors is Professor Jesse Lutabingwa of Appalachian State University. He was the director of the Mandela Washington Fellowship (MWF) program at the school. Amidst all 25 Mandela Washington Fellows, I was the only one who asked for mentorship and unexpectedly he agreed.

2. Maximize the opportunities that you have to learn from your mentor: I have sat with Jesse only four (4) times since 2017, but those four (4) times were defining moments for me. He advised me to pivot Sozo Networks into a leadership development institute. So, from just working with teenagers, we are now

known for leading and training an ecosystem of young social change makers. Jesse Lutabingwa developed the curriculum and training for our grant writing course and took the online course. This course has been a major source of revenue for Sozo Networks over the years. Mentors may not always be available but maximize every single time you have with them.

3. Choose a mentor whose path aligns with yours: stand on his/her shoulders and you will see farther than him/her. I leverage my mentors' experiences to make better decisions. I often ask them about their failures and regrets. I ask about circumstances/actions that led to their success and failures. Some of their responses have helped me in carefully making both personal decisions like who to marry and professional decisions like choosing a career path.

4. Three years ago, all I could ever see myself doing was helping young people in Ibadan but Jesse and Rev Eboda helped me to realize I could do a lot more. My mentors forced me to create a vision and actionable steps with milestones. Jesse convinced me to go back to school for my masters, he encouraged me to go for my PhD and wrote mind-blowing recommendations for me.

5. The mentee drives the mentor-mentee relationship: As a mentee, I have to keep showing up, booking appointments, and keep engaging them meaningfully. One way I have engaged some of my mentors is to ask them to serve on the board of my organisation. This way I have more access to them and I am able to better leverage their networks and resources.

MENTORSHIP PREPARES YOU FOR LIFE CHALLENGES

DISU KAMOR
(Executive Director, MPAC)

My personal experience with mentoring actually predated my professional career period. I had a unique experience during my secondary school days to be mentored by a teacher who invested his time and energy to nurture me to excel in my studies with a marked impression. This period was remarkable for me because looking back at this period in my life, it is clear that the opportunity I had with the mentorship experience set my foot on a different path that ultimately led to a fresh experience for me. The defining relationship I had with the mentor at this stage in my life made me realise the important impacts of investing in the lives of those we can influence.

In my career life, I have also had the opportunity to mentor people and to be mentored. The experience for me created a much deeper sense of trust and enabled better communication which had transformation on both work and life. I was able to influence mentees through my life values and took important lessons and opportunities in developing soft skills which have helped me again, on and off the job. Some of them are life skills that continue to work for me outside the work environment. I would say that some of the important lessons I have picked up during the mentorship opportunities that I have had, have prepared me well for challenges in life better than some valuable lessons I have picked up in some structured learning environment.

ATTRACT MENTORS BY DISCIPLINE, HARD WORK, CONSISTENCY AND SHOWING UP

HAMMED KAYODE ALABI

(Sub-Saharan Africa Representative for Peace First and Founder KLCI)

I have always been someone who really doesn't run around asking people to mentor me. I follow people who I feel I can learn from and graciously learn from afar. I have been doing this for a very long time and I keep putting in the work. I do not rush to people and I don't just call people my mentor. Mentorship is intentional. I connect with people I am looking to learn from on social media and I kept doing my work silently and sharing on social media. They can keep track of what I am doing and whenever I reach out or request for mentorship, they do not turn me down. They know I am result driven and no one would want to turn down a star. When I joined Sozo as a volunteer in 2017, it didn't take so much time to learn from the founder, Segun Fatudimu.

I am always interested in the cause of my mentors; I contribute and sacrifice - it's a two-way process. So, the mentorship was easy, it was experiential and I was able to transfer some of the things I learned from him to what I was doing in my initiatives. This is the same way I have connected with powerful people in the non-profit space like Adepeju Jaiyeoba etc.

For me, sharing my work has been key and it allows me to attract not just mentors but sponsors. Apart from this, it gave me an opportunity to also inspire some other people too and that got me to serve as a mentor for the Diana Award in the UK."

WHEN THERE IS NO MENTOR

AISHA ADAMS
(Founder, Sidiqqah Street Kitchen)

I didn't really have Mentors per se. I just sort of winged it, made my mistakes and grew. However, mentoring others has made me more responsible and accountable.

I take my responsibility quite seriously and whenever I am placed in a position of leadership, I am conscious of my role to shape others through my actions and/or inactions so I always held myself to high standards.

This put quite a strain on me, however being self-disciplined and optimistic seemed to cushion the effects of the strain.

One of my biggest motivations in life has always been my intent to leave my footprints in the sands of time and you don't do so by doing ordinary things and setting standards that anyone can scale through. My leadership style was to be harder on myself than I was on others. So, if I wouldn't compromise even when I need it; what's your excuse?

I also rarely ever do shortcuts. I apply myself to things, I get my hands dirty. I work harder than I ask others to work. I have been dubbed "the workaholic", "machine" and other titles by those who have worked closely with me. Therefore, I would say that the willingness to learn and pick myself up every time I made errors helped me. Optimism, commitment to learning, open-mindedness to constructive feedback and most importantly, praying harder than I work have supported me on my growth journey. I usually would say to them; the dream is the focus and it is bigger than us all.

So, commitment to a worthy cause with utmost sincerity and intentionality has supported the growth journey as well.

***Mr. Disu Kamor is not a Millenial.**

STORYTELLING AND OPPORTUNITIES

TELL TO WIN- THE ART OF PURPOSEFUL STORYTELLING IN APPLICATIONS AND IN BUSINESS

ONYEDIKACHI EKWERIKE

Think right now about the story you heard growing up as a child, the one story that basically stuck with you growing up. Why did this story stick with you? What made it powerful?

Mutiat, a participant in the mentorship program, shared the story of her birth and the challenges her parents experienced as narrated by her late dad. Her dad was a medical doctor. As a doctor, he had clear plans for his wife's birth experience to ensure safe delivery. He had everything planned to the tee; he was a man who liked to be in control of situations involving his family. Mutiat came into the world on 1st of January, two days earlier than her Expected Date of Delivery. Things were not going to plan.

On the day she was born, her mother ate some wraps of pounded yam, which was assumed to have induced her labour. Hoping to handle the birth himself, Mutiat's dad drove her Mum to the hospital. In haste, he forgot the keys to the room where his equipment was stored. Once he noticed he was without the keys, he rushed back home to get them. On his way home, he drove his car into a ditch. Things were not going to plan. He had planned to be there, at his wife's side, ensuring the safe birth of his daughter, but here he was stuck with the car in a ditch.

Although there were some complications, the delivery was not too difficult, as Mutiat made her appearance at 5:30am, just about time for the Muslim call to prayer. Meanwhile, her dad was still stuck in the ditch. It was not until around 6am when a passerby saw him and helped him out. Mutiat heard this story time and time again as she grew up. Her dad will tell this story every time she goes through a difficult challenge, to remind her that she was resilient, and that she always found a way to make things happen and overcome despite challenges. The last time she heard her dad tell this story, she was 13, shortly before he passed away. Although her dad is no more, this story sticks with her and acts as a reminder to persevere even when things do not go to plan.

Stories are powerful. The stories we have been told, along with those we tell ourselves, shape who we are and how we see the world. Mutiat's resilience stems from repeatedly being told about the story of her birth. And in times of difficulties, she draws strength from that story to keep going. What are some stories you tell yourself that helps you to keep going?

Stories are valuable and easy to recollect. If you remember nothing at all from this text, I am positive you will remember Mutiat's story. You will remember the woman who picked her own time to arrive into the world. You will remember how her father got stuck in a ditch and could not be at his wife's side, even though he did all he could to prepare for it. We will remember that Mutiat draws strength from this story and it has made her into the resilient woman she is today.

Stories help to build connection. The next time you write an application for a fellowship program, or a grant proposal, tell your story. Marshall Ganz, a professor at Havard calls this the story of self. This story of self shows why you have been called to do what you have been called to. Sharing personal stories requires a measure of vulnerability. However, being vulnerable allows people connect with us, and stories are the vehicles that drive that connection.

Imagine right now that Mutiat puts in an application for a fellowship program, and in that application, she tells this story of her birth. And, at the end of the story, she connects it to how she has been able to succeed from time to time despite significant challenges. She shares how she rose from hardship, losing her dad at only 13 and states how she draws from her birth story to keep going in the face of difficulties. Anyone who reads that application will feel inspired and connected to Mutiat.

So how do we go about crafting a winning application using stories? Traditionally, good stories have five elements; characters, plot, setting, conflict and resolution. Characters are individuals in the story. Describe details of the character, so your audience can picture them in their minds. The plot is the gist of the story itself, it should have a clear beginning, middle and end. The setting is where the events take place. The conflict is the challenges and problems the character faces, it is the core of the plot. Lastly, resolution is the action taken by the character to overcome the challenge. Telling stories in your applications is not quite the same as writing a book or a movie. So, all five components do not have to be fully developed.

A good application or personal statement should have three components; Introduction, Body, and Conclusion. Your story should typically be in your introduction. Your story itself should also have a beginning, a middle part and a conclusion.

INTRODUCTION

Powerful introductions often utilize a device called attention getters. An attention getter is anything that helps you capture the focus of your audience. This could be a question, joke, shocking statistic or a short narrative/story. This is where the art of storytelling comes in. In my experience, I have found that narratives are very powerful attention getters, for reasons mentioned above. They help to create connections.

For example, if I was applying for a Doctoral scholarship at a university to study Clinical Psychology and I was crafting my personal statement, I could begin by sharing a personal story of how helpless I felt when a relative suffered postpartum depression (Character). Next, I could share how it was hard to find an organization who provided women with support in Nigeria (Conflict), and how Nigeria is overly religious and people believe mental illnesses are spiritual attacks (Setting), how my family members treated her poorly, and the suffering she endured (Plot). Lastly, I could share how I decided to do something about it by advocating for her to get professional help and creating an organization that raises awareness about postpartum depression (Resolution). I will then connect this story to my application by stating that my work has inspired me to learn more about clinical psychology and my PhD research will revolve around understanding predictors of postpartum depression among Nigerian women.

Sharing a personal story like this can be hard as it requires you to be vulnerable. However, like I mentioned earlier, this story helps to build connection with your reader and helps them see why you are passionate about your work.

Secondly, your story should have audience relevance. Include in your story statements that help your audience see how they are affected by the issues you are passionate about. Going back to my story on why I am passionate about psychology and my research on postpartum depression, I could add that our society depends greatly on our mothers. If our mothers are not mentally healthy, it affects the child's socio-emotional development. We would not want a society where individuals grow to be adults who are not well adjusted. Statements like these help the readers see why my work is important and how it impacts them.

BODY

The body of your application or personal statement should contain all the other technical things about you. Your professional experiences and academic background. Talk yourself up. This is not the time to be humble, give yourself license to blow your own trumpet. If you do not hype yourself, who will?

CONCLUSION

Your conclusion should be as powerful as your introduction. Why so? This is because people often will remember the first and last things you say or the first and last things they read. In psychology, it is called the Primacy and Recency effect. Do you recall when you were a child and had to learn the alphabets? You might recall that it was easier for you to remember A,B,C,D and X,Y,Z. I know personally that this was the case with me. I will always find myself "chewing my mouth" when I get to the alphabets in the middle, but I never struggled to remember ABCD and XYZ. This is how our memory works. We often remember the first and last things in any message people share with us.

In your conclusion, review your main points. You could do this by simply saying "up to this point, I have shared xyz". Once you have reviewed your main points, end with a clincher. For instance, in my application, I can end by saying "what will become of a society that does not care for the mental health of our moms? My research will enable me to understand how we can better support the mental health of our mothers. Maternal mental health matters!"

Finally, be authentic. Tell your own story, do not appropriate other people's stories. Use and trust your own voice. No one can tell your story better than you. Do not exaggerate, tell your truth. When you tell your story, your reader is better able to see why you are passionate about what you do.

One of the things that drew me to Ahmad was the story he shared with me about why he got involved in the work he does today, which involves advocating for prisoners' rights.

He said, "When I was in the university, I think in 200 level, I went to the prison for the first time. On that visit we had inmates narrate their reason for ending up in prison. A lot of them mentioned that at that point in time, they didn't have lawyers because they couldn't afford one. In my naivety, I had promised that when I become a lawyer, I will come back. I didn't really hold it to heart. However, in the course of my National Youth Service in Abia State, one of the places I volunteered in was the prison. My outstanding services there got me the best youth corps member award. Upon completing my NYSC and returning to Lagos, I wanted to convince myself that I put in so much not just because of the award but because I was deeply motivated to assist people.

After my youth service, I connected with a chaplain in the Prison through an Islamic Organization. When we went to the prison, I interviewed the first set of people I met and I successfully secured their release. There was the motivation to do more. So, when you ask why I do what I am doing, I would say, it was because of the initial promise I made to the inmates when I visited them as a student."

His story demonstrates why he is committed to the work he is doing. His experience during NYSC and the promise he made to the inmates he encountered in Abia State, inspired him.

What is your story? Why does the work you do matter to you? Tell it, the world is waiting!

WINNING HACK: HOW TO WRITE WINNING APPLICATIONS FOR SCHOLARSHIP AND FELLOWSHIP OPPORTUNITIES

HAMMED KAYODE ALABI

There is no gainsaying the fact that fellowships and scholarships are highly coveted opportunities that complement other factors to build a bright future for anyone.

How can we position ourselves to win at least one Fellowship/Scholarship?

My Story
I can recall having a lot of experience in the development space. I joined the Nigerian Red Cross Society at the University, facilitated free tutorials for less intelligent students in my department. I served as an HIV and AIDS peer educator, carried out six community development projects as a corps member during my National Youth Service Corps scheme while being a volunteer at the Girl Child Foundation. When I was fifteen, I started teaching in a rural basic school in Lagos and still did not know there were opportunities out there to catalyse.

Upon realising the opportunities inherent in my achievements, I started to scout for opportunities in fellowships and scholarships. I failed woefully in the first application I submitted, and I have had up to thirty rejections or more. I learned the hard way.
The good thing is that you won't have to make the same mistakes I made if you understand the four things about writing winning essays. These are Storytelling, Impact, Numbers, and Focus.

Benefits of Fellowships and Scholarships
1.   They position you for a career in international and global development.
2.   They give you the opportunity to network with amazing young leaders across the world.
3.   They boost your confidence level as they help you to learn from dynamic individuals and cultural competencies.
4.   They help you develop local, regional and international competencies.
5.   They enable you to access relevant mentors in your field of expertise.
6.   They are your fastest route to building a career in academics and becoming a consultant by proving you already have years of experience on the field.

Tips Required for Winning Fellowships and Scholarships

Winning a fellowship and scholarship isn't as hard as people think it is. You need to follow certain principles that will give you an edge over other applicants. Here are two important requirements for creating a winning fellowship and scholarship.

1.   Research

Before turning in your application, you have to research the organisation or program you are applying to. That's the first step. Read about their values and know what they stand for. Also, find alumni of such programs and reach out to them for helpful insights. They may help with application reviews and give you first-hand information.

2. **Eligibility**

    Many applications are rejected even before they get a chance to be read. Before applying, you have to check out for the eligibility. Check for age, experience, passion, specificity and track record. Apply for the ones you are qualified for. However, some applications require you to have minimal experience. In fact, some are looking for people who are yet to be made.

- Tidy up your application: Don't be in a hurry to submit your application once you're done preparing it. You want to spend some time tidying up your application to ensure the accuracy of the information you provided. So before you do the final submission, do these:

- Proofread: Write your application beforehand in a Word Document and you may use an application like Grammarly to proofread. You don't want your essay to appear rough and untidy. It has to connect and make a lot of sense.

- Remove irrelevant statements: Be focused, do not write about too many things, although you may write more than the required number initially and later sieve it. Remove all irrelevant statements. Every word must count.

Other important tips include:

- Starting your application early to meet up with the deadline.
- Breaking down the elements of each question and being vulnerable in telling your story. Do not be too humble while doing so, it is an opportunity to blow your trumpet.

- Getting a friend or someone within your close network to read. Sometimes, they see what you do not see.
- Do not dwell too much on it, once you feel you are through, submit.

Examples of Application Questions and Rules for Answering Them

Here, I will use Carrington Fellowship as a case study and I will also pick some random application questions from other scholarship applications too.

Question 1 - Briefly describe your duties at your current job or what you are currently studying. (100-word limit)

Guide - Please, go straight to the point here. You do not need to start talking about multiple roles. If you are a student, talk briefly about what you are studying and your role as a student. Despite the fact that I had started my initiative, I decided not to talk about it in my application. Rather, I chose to describe my volunteer manager role, a role I performed at Sozo Networks.

My response:

I am the volunteer manager at Sozo Networks Lagos on the project tagged "Before I turn 18". The "Before I turn 18" project is a project that prepares teenagers for leadership before they turn 18. I also help in recruiting volunteers.

Talk about your duties. Simple as that. Please do not forget the word count. For me, I used all the 100 here.

In some applications, it will tell you to write about yourself, why do you do what you do? Go straight to the point too!

I start this way most times:

"I have had twelve years of experience in active citizenship and volunteering! I lost my mum at seven, my dad became unemployed at the same time, so I also stayed out-of-school for a whole academic term and this inspired me to start Kayode Alabi Leadership and Career Initiative, where I empower young people in rural communities to…"

Question 2- Why do you want to be as a CYFI Fellow (100-word limit)

Many of us should be familiar with this question. Why do you want to be selected as a Mandela Washington Fellow? You have to study the fellowship to study what you will learn? Why do you want the MasterCard Scholarship? What do they stand for? What organisation do they partner with? What activities will you do?

Guide - It is very important here to know what the fellowship offers and how it aligns with what you want and the skills you want to develop via the programme.

For instance, you can say, "I want to learn community mobilization techniques, personal performance enhancement techniques, leadership and public speaking skills. I want to connect with other young leaders etc."

In my application, I even talked about how I look forward to contributing to curriculum development and reviewing the Education Policy. Actually, I was targeting the education team. So, I knew what I wanted from the beginning.

Question 3- Please describe a past social impact project that you helped implement, please focus on your specific contribution to the project. (250 words or less)

In some cases, tell us how you have demonstrated leadership.

Guide - Here, they want to know how you have demonstrated leadership and your specific contribution. This may range from an NYSC project to a school project. You have to realize that any project is good enough, however small. It may even be a sanitation programme in your area. I address such a question using the STAR Model.

S- Situation
T - Task
A - Action
R - Result

"Situation" could be described using data or observation.

My response:

Only nine out of ten people who grew up in an underserved community end up having a meaningful career in the future. This is the same situation in the Makoko community, a popular slum in Lagos. As a young corps member who served in this community, I an three other corps members fundraised $500 and executed a career *guidance programme which lasted for a week. I taught basic life skills such as leadership, critical thinking and teamwork. These are skills needed for the future of work. At the end of the training, 250 students were reached within the community and were placed on mentorship which occurs once in every month within the community. One of the success stories is James Godwin who started a skills club in his school to train others on what he learned in the programme.*

In some applications, they will ask you what project are you currently working on?

It's either you look at a project you are part of or a project you are carrying out within an organisation or a personal project.

i.   Elements of the question?

ii.   What is the problem statement?

iii. What is the solution?

iv.   What will be the proposed impact and numbers you will reach?

Example

Today, youths between ages fifteen and twenty-four account for 20% of Sub-Saharan Africa's total population. According to the United Nations Development Programmes (2017), they are almost two hundred million, thus making them the largest generation the region has ever raised. We believe these young people are the solutions to our problems and not the cause. They have great ideas but are not heard.

As a Fellow-in-Residence with Peace First, I currently lead a project called "The Peace First Challenge" where I recruit under-resourced young people between thirteen and twenty-five years in Sub-Saharan Africa through stories and in partnership with youth-led organisations. We support their ideas and aid in solving problems in their community. I help deepen their knowledge about the injustice they want to solve and assist them in creating a solution grounded in compassion, courage and collaboration. I provide feedback on their plans and budget and approve a mini-grant up to $250 in bringing these ideas into reality. I provide additional mentorship via skype. I also help them understand the sustainability of their ideas after which I connect them with regional resources to enable them to develop their leadership potential in the region. Currently, I support and have recruited over two hundred young people from thirty Sub-Saharan African countries who are working to address access to quality education, insecurity, health services, poverty, and civic engagement. I have distributed $250 to thirty young people working to address these issues. My target is to distribute a hundred mini-grants before the end of June 2020.

This is one of my personal essays that got me into a prestigious scholarship interview!

Question 4: What challenges have you faced, how did you overcome the challenges and what did you learn?

Elements of the question:

- Challenges you have faced.
- How did you overcome it?

LESSONS

Again, you need to use the STAR model

My Response:

After graduating from the University and completing the National Youth Service, I got a job to work as an examination invigilator in Saudi Arabia for 2 years while I was on the verge of starting my NGO. My annual income would be $6000 but I turned it down to continue my work in youth activism and volunteering. This decision didn't go down well with my family. During this period, I was motivated to take online courses such as "Community Organizing for Action", from the Young African Leadership Initiative platform and attended the Regional Leadership Centre Funded by Mastercard Foundation. I participated in a lot of youth development programmes, one of which was the First African Youth SDGs Summit in Accra, Ghana. I connected with African Monitor where I worked as a Youth Champion, I travelled through 3 regions, 12 communities and engaged over 600 ordinary citizens in Nigeria on development issues such as poverty, education, gender equality etc. The report from the engagement gave me an opportunity to engage the Senate President on sustainable development. I also created a blog www.kayfactorinspires.com, where I use storytelling to connect people to issues that affect them. I got into the Carrington Fellowship, won $5000, created the first learning management system for teachers (www.teachingedge.org) in Nigeria and then won the U.S Consul General Award and the African Youth Essay competition award. That one decision changed my whole life, paving the way to a life of national and regional impact.

This is a similar response that I submitted to the MasterCard Scholarship Program and a similar fellowship. Please do not duplicate this essay or use it.

The key thing here is that you should also share what you have learned from the challenges you are currently facing.

Another response would be:

During my NYSC I wanted to construct a volleyball court that would serve over 5000 youths in Ekpon village in Edo State but resources were limited. I noticed that the community members were not financially capable. So, I thought about what I could replace with money. First, I identified key stakeholders and development organisations within the community. I attended their meetings and pitched my idea. I also noticed the community had free sand, I worked with two youths to pack them and the community saw the passion and the king summoned me. And I was supported with up to $300. I also raised an extra $400 through a personal network and the court was constructed partnering with local bricklayers. Currently, there is a reduction in vices and young people within the community are engaged via sports. That single act showed me the power of "lead by example" and using domestic resource mobilization to create change.

PS: I used this during my Carrington Fellowship Interview. I have discovered that Fellowship Application is storytelling and this; I have learned about the act. So, guys go on and write that winning essay!

The truth is that it's not as if we are not the best but there are just a lot of people competing for very few spots. So you need to keep building capacity, keep building the necessary networks, keep volunteering and doing the real work. One day, your door will open and it is just one opportunity that would change your whole life.

Sometimes, you don't even need the Mandela Washington Fellowship to catalyse. There are some fellowships out there, like the current fellowship I am currently in, I have travelled to two countries already. Missed my trip to London and India due to visa issues and COVID-19. I am also working with a global non-profit and do you know what that means? I currently sit with the Director of Asoka and world leaders as a learning leader in a particular global community. You only need one door to open up for you; don't give up, keep fighting and doing the work. If you are not doing anything, you would not have a story to tell. Do something!!!

QUESTION AND ANSWER SESSION

1.   How easy is it to get selected for fellowship/scholarship, as most things in Nigeria are connection inclined?

Response: The truth is that most people who coordinate the fellowship/scholarships are not Nigerians and there is no connection. Just do your best and you will shine through. More importantly, stay true to your core and be able to articulate your why and tell the story. And there are some Nigerian programmes that are not biased too, please do not allow this kind of mindset deny you of boundless opportunities. All the opportunities I have got, I did not connect with anyone or know someone.

2. My question is for people who do not have a formal or organised community service portfolio or documented volunteering activities. How do you navigate the application especially if you're passionate about adding value but never saw the importance of keeping records?

Response: I think it's wise to document some of your activities. However, if you can't, like I don't document everything maybe because I share on social media and have a telegraphic memory. One thing you need to do is to pay attention to your story, just find a moment to brainstorm and reflect on the little you have done and then share that little.

Most times, the selection committee can identify your passion and no story is useless. You can even talk about your leadership experience in primary school. Let me tell a story with that:

As a young boy at age 9, I was selected as a senior prefect, that was my first taste of leadership. During this period, students bully others in the class and cause disorderliness, and as the head prefect, I quickly devised a means to checkmate this. I gave the opportunity to bullies to head projects in my class because I noticed they are looking for an opportunity to lead. Since then, bullying reduced by 70% and there was a peaceful coexistence in my class. This single act has shaped my leadership potential and I have always thought of engaging people who share different perspectives from me.

P.S: This story is fictitious. I just made it up. It's a good example of how you can weave your leadership experience from the past.

3. I'm a Corps member presently and I want to deliver a SMART

project with my individual Community Development Service (CDS). How do I go about it?

Response: First observe the community, conduct a need assessment and identify the problems they are facing. What are the root causes of these problems? What can you do to solve their problems? What resources do you need? How can you access those resources? If resources are limited, how many people can you reach? Instead of 1000, why not 50. Instead of the whole community, why not just a quarter of the community.

4.   What is the idea of fellowship and why is it something we should long for?

Response: Fellowship helps you to develop yourself professionally. Every fellowship has aims and objectives. You have to ensure the aim aligns with your career trajectory. For instance, the Carrington fellowship is for emerging social impact leaders/social entrepreneurs, you have the opportunity of building key skills in the space to catalyse. Some of the skills are passed on to other work and you are more positioned and prepared for a particular career. It may be the breaking point for you and the people you connect with, you become friends for life.

5.   Does one need to have many years of managing a project before one can apply?

Response: Not at all, they will specify what they want. Even if you have done only a little, share your little experience and be proud of it.

6.   I have an NGO that deals with teenagers and being a Muslim female, do you think that grant is not sex or religion segmented and also what's the percentage of grant issued compared to applications?

Response: It is not religion segmented. I have seen someone who attended a Carrington Interview with her hijab and she got in.

7.   I recall you lamenting your rejection in some scholarships you applied for last year. You have just been selected for a prestigious scholarship with another one on the way, having made the final stage and performed creditably well. How were you able to use your rejections as a springboard to success? What did you do to change the cause of things from rejection to being sought after?

Response: I think, first, I was not telling my story well. I have got so many opportunities like Carrington Fellowship and all but I was not talking about it. I have attended programmes and spoke at regional levels but I was not sharing them. So, I noticed I was not raw enough and vulnerable in telling my story. I decided to change strategy, I was more vulnerable and I was able to articulate my stories properly. I also worked more. Whenever you get rejected, it should inspire you to do more. I had access to another major opportunity as a fellow-in-residence with Peace First and my work with them added to my portfolio. I also added all my work experience from day one since 2008 up to date. I didn't do that previously, many things changed within a year and I was able to communicate the change. A lot can change in one year.

8.   Are there age limits to applying for any of these scholarships?

Response: Chevening, I think, does not have an age limit and Commonwealth Scholarship doesn't as well. I can recall, a friend of mine said his mum got the Commonwealth scholarship. I was like your mum?!! He said if his mum can get it, He can too. He has been nominated this year. MasterCard and some other ones are age bound.

9.   What if you feel you don't have enough story to tell about yourself. Probably, you don't have any project you have done, does it mean you can never get a scholarship?

Response: Some scholarships might not require experience e.g. Commonwealth in some cases. However, you should be able to communicate your career plan and what you hope to do. What will you do for the first five years, fifteen years later and long-term?

I am sure having a bit of volunteering experience would give one an edge, it is never too late to build our story.

The truth is, it is not that we have not done so much but probably we did not pay attention to those little things we have done. Some of us were prefects in our secondary schools or primary schools. Some of us did a bit of politics at the university and we created changes and some of us did group or personal community development services during our NYSC years. This forms our uniqueness and who we are. We need to sit down to reflect and see how we can weave all of these stories together. The truth is that no story is too small to share and change doesn't necessarily have to be something big. Even when I started my NGO and we had just reached one hundred and fifty with only three volunteers, I still talked about my work and shared my story.

The key thing here is your "why". How do you weave it to what you are currently doing?

So, there is no late or early time and we can start now. Take courses online; there was a time in 2016 when I took 15 courses in 3 days. Start a blog to talk about your work or area of interest. You know if you are interested in Microbiology, what problem do you intend to solve? How would you use blogging to solve it? Medium and blogger.com allow you to create a free blog and you can curate your stories. In my blog today, I have over 100,000 views from 12 countries. The blog has been existing since 2017. Imagine that you are sharing knowledge there, you appear as an expert. In addition, you have to start looking for volunteering opportunities. Some would say, "we have searched and searched". Try the smaller NGOs and volunteer with them. Grow with them and they'll position you for opportunities. Remember that "day one" is different from "one day". To achieve "one day", you have to start from "day one".

Go and start!

SOME FELLOWSHIPS AND SCHOLARSHIPS YOU CAN APPLY TO:

1. Mandela Washington Fellowship
    (https://yaliapp.irex.org/Logon?ReturnUrl=%2f)
    Application Timeline: September - October

2. Carrington Youth Fellowship Initiative (Lagos)
    (https://www.cyfinigeria.org/)
    Application Timeline: January - February

3. Young African Leadership Initiative Regional Leadership Centre (Accra Ghana)
    (https://yaliwestafrica.net/rlc/index.php/apply-nowsdafawfwqr/)
    Application timeline: On a quarterly basis

4. Peace First Mini-Grant up to $250 (13 - 25 years)
    (https://www.peacefirst.org/)
    Application timeline: Rolling basis

5. Pollination Grant up to $1000
    (https://thepollinationproject.org/)
    Application timeline: Rolling basis

6. IDS Graduate Scholarship (Masters in Development Studies) University of Sussex. Alumni have to apply directly to the University.

7. Chevening Scholarship
    (https://www.chevening.org/scholarship/nigeria/) (For any
    Masters Program)
    Application Timeline: August - November

8. MasterCard Foundation Scholarship University of Edinburgh

9. MasterCard Foundation Scholarship McGill Yarn University,
    and many more Commonwealth Scholarship &
    Commonwealth Shared Scholarship (September - December)

BUSINESS

PREPARING YOUR BUSINESS FOR FINANCIAL GROWTH

KABIRU OLANREWAJU

Business Planning is the process of determining an enterprise's objectives, strategies and projected actions in order to promote its survival and development within a given time frame.

A business plan is the plan made by an entity to look ahead, allocate resources, focus on key points, and prepare for challenges and opportunities.
This has two main features: Profit/(Loss) Making and Risks Mitigation.

Business Planning is not an end in itself, rather a means to an end. To achieve this end, an appraisal process must be included in the Business Planning cycle.

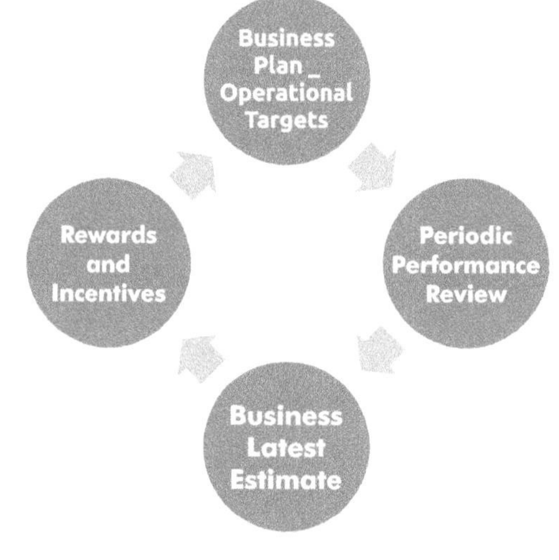

Periodic Performance appraisal, on one hand, concentrates on the execution of the strategic and operating plans. The Latest Estimate (LE) exercise aims to give a realistic and accurate representation of where the organization will end the period vs initial plan given the latest view of the business environment.

Budgeting, on the other hand, is a vital process in determining the amount of funding required to run the entity's business plan in any given period. It is vital in ensuring that scarce resources are allocated to areas where it will deliver the most value.

This exercise is usually preferred to be done based on activity type.

Your organization's Budgeting and Planning team is expected to play a critical role in coordinating and integrating the various business functions to successfully deliver competitive and credible business plans, whilst also driving the appraisal of those plans to ensure alignment to strategic objectives for all stakeholders.

Some Features of a Good Plan

- Assumptions must have sound bases that can be supported by achievements in similar conditions.
- Risks must be identified and incorporated in the plan.
- How far away from historical performance is the plan. [Historical performance must be considered in drawing the plan.]
- Did you achieve your plans in the past? [Success rates of previous plans must be factored into the new plan]

Risks include:

- **Technical risks** depend on your area of operation. What could go wrong that your technical skills will not be able to manage.

- **Economic risks** include financial, fiscal (e.g. rate of taxation change), interest rate exposure, foreign exchange movement, price, credit, liquidity, accounting and reporting,
- **Commercial risks** include procurements, rights and obligations related to agreements, changes to market share, default of a significant vendor, etc.
- **Political risks** include changes in governments, communities, partners, and shareholders as well as risks relating to regulatory approval.

Why do you need to do all these stressful works?

- This is critical as it is a major ingredient of any organization's Control Framework.
- This helps you to understand what resources are required to run your organization.
- It is also a critical requirement when funding is being sourced from whether grants giving organizations, investors or even credit providers.
- It makes the organization become resilient and helps put its "house" in order.

Methods of Planning:

1. Top-Down method.
2. Bottoms-Up method.

Top-Down method.

In this method, you start with your organizational target for the year and work down the details of what is required to achieve it.

Benefits:

It can stretch you beyond your imagination.

Demerits:

It could be discouraging if you could not secure the resources required to achieve the outcome.

Bottoms-Up method.

In this method, you collate what is required in each department and work out the outcome it will generate for the organization at the end of the period.

Benefits:

Ownership is easier.

Demerits:

The organization may not grow as fast as its potential.

It is advisable to use a mix of the two approaches from time to time with the Top-Down approach considered to be a bit better.

BUILDING ORGANISATIONAL STRUCTURES AND FOSTERING PARTNERSHIPS

DISU KAMOR

Today, we are talking about an organisation in terms of commercial activities. When setting up an organisational structure, there should be an objective on what is to be done and the various units that will be involved in achieving the objective must have a defined line of responsibilities.

When the units have a clear definition of their roles, it makes the organisational structure better equipped to function effectively.

You need to have your organogram, target and interdependence of the units. You have to know where demand, respect, responsibility and accountability starts.

Fostering Partnerships

The main aspect I am speaking on is collaboration. I believe that human diversity is a blessing from God and needs to be harnessed for the benefit of everyone as is seen in the capitalist world.

Collaboration is people coming together to achieve something. Collaboration is basically teamwork taken to the next level.

Professor Bill Mohill observed that there were some chickens with ability to lay more eggs than others so he took them to a place together with others who are low performers and allowed them to stay together for a year (12 months) and found out the following:

1. The chickens who are high performers reduced greatly in numbers due to hostile environment e.g. red zone chickens

2. The chickens with average/low performance grew healthier, grew by 500% e.g. green zone chickens.

The high-performance chickens couldn't survive the environment. So as organisations, we need to do all we can to develop collaborative skills.

Businesses are now adopting the Coopetition (Cooperation + Competition) strategy. This is very common in the Automobile Industry where two rival automobile manufacturers make the most of their complementary competencies, enjoy economies of scale (by sharing suppliers, distributors and even production lines) and speed up innovation. As individuals, it's natural to have our personal inclinations and aspirations but when we cooperate, we harness the strength of everyone together.

We also need to build culture and collaborative skills for our organisation and one of the important ways we can achieve this is through fundraising.

Fundraising

To Fundraise effectively;

- Set SMART goals.
- Map out your network very well: engage in activities that will increase your visibility.

- Identify and find your advocates.
- Be visible online.
- Be transparent as an organisation and report your organisation's activities to the public as well as regulators.

Certain tips to create Collaboration

- Persuade and encourage team members to claim ownership of the set goals.
- Empower all team members to generate and suggest ideas (interdependence) and assume the best of each other.
- Clear yourself of every negative trait.
- Have a clear understanding of set visions.
- Create fun while working.
- Recognise and celebrate your successes and recognise and acknowledge the failures to avoid them in future.

OVERCOMING SETBACKS AND RUNNING A PROFITABLE SOCIAL ENTERPRISE

USMAN ALLI LAWAN (Farmer in Suit)

Every young entrepreneur wants to achieve success. Success is often measured by how much profit your enterprise makes and how much impact you are making in society. The question most young people ask me is, how do you manage your business in a way that it is profitable? However, what I think many young entrepreneurs should learn is how to bounce back from setbacks and how to make social impact with their business.

My name is USMAN Alli Lawan. They call me the Farmer in suit. The Farmer in suit was built organically. I didn't "blow" overnight. The farmer in suit has been in the making for over 35 years. But professionally, the Farmer in suit metamorphosed in the last seven (7) years.

When I was young, I just wanted to be rich. When I was in university, I didn't understand the CGPA system. I didn't know that I needed a 2.1' to be able to make something with my university degree. I was just studying. Thankfully, I had an upbringing that taught me to be able to live the triangular life- school, mosque, home. I actually only began to understand the CGPA system during my final year. If I was an unserious student who only realized that he was making a 3rd class in his final year, it would have been fatal.

After university, I set out to serve and I wanted to serve in Lagos and more importantly, I wanted to serve in a Bank, which I did. It was in

Intercontinental Bank. Before I clocked 26 years, I was already writing CRS (Credit Reserve Summary) for up to 500 million naira in the Bank. Generally, you are not allowed to write CRS of 100 million naira until you have served for at least five years in a Bank. A lot of factors were involved. I had mentors who were my bosses, who wanted me to do well and of course, I was committed.

I worked in the Bank for some years and then moved into the Oil and Gas sector. Remember, all of this was premised on one goal- The goal of making money. By the time I turned 26, I was worth over 2 million dollars (150 million naira at that time).

I thought I had made it. I began to burn the money like wildfire. I associated with the wrong people and went to the wrong places. I was lost, nothing seemed right. I had a lot of money, but I had no purpose. I was scared of being poor, I lived my life trying to prove to people that I was rich. Then the financial crises of 2008-2009 happened. When it came, it hit my business like a bomb. In less than 10 Days, we saw the price of oil, specifically diesel, fall from 126 naira per litre to 72 naira per litre. Automatically what that means is if you have a 100 million naira in the Oil and gas sector, naturally by the Economic Force Majeure, your holding drops by 50 percent. So, in less than 10 days, you are worth only 50 million naira.
Now, because we were not prepared and didn't expect the crisis, I had no previous experience, nor the guidance of mentors, I struggled. Every move we made to salvage the situation exacerbated the problems. It was like I was sinking in a quicksand and that was how someone who was worth 2 million dollars at the age of 26, became broke, broken and homeless at the age of 29.

So, I went out to develop myself by getting a degree at university in the UK. Again, when I went to the UK, I went with the hope that when

I get back to Nigeria, I will be able to get employment in the Oil and Gas sector. My aspirations influenced my choice of course of study which was Energy studies, specifically, I majored in Energy Finance. I came back to Nigeria and there was no Job, shocker. The Oil and Gas guru, with an advanced degree from the UK, couldn't secure a job or a place to stay. I was sinking.

Then I started leveraging my friends and my network. Between January 2012 to July 2012, I sent out more than 500 applications whether there was an opening or not. I took up lecturing at a university in my home state for a couple of months, but because I sent out multiple applications, I got a call to come in for an interview from a World Bank project. I did the interview and was selected for the job. I informed the Dean of faculty at the university that I was leaving. The Dean told me that he understood my decision to leave and that it was okay. He said it was something he would have done if he was in my shoes. However, he advised that I reflect on why I was making the decision to leave, to be sure that I was not just leaving for the money, to be sure that I was taking the job with World Bank because it aligned with my purpose. Money should never be the motive, strive for opportunities that aligns with your purpose.

I took the Job. I remembered calling my mentor and telling him about my plans and the money World Bank was offering. My plans were simple and clear; Work for one year, get my life together, and start a new business of my own.

In my heart, I knew I needed a plan, but this time it had to be different, it had to be a plan that is consistent with my purpose. So, I started searching for what my purpose is. For a start, I set up a small poultry farm with 300 Birds. As I ran this farm, I made a lot of mistakes, but I did well to learn from them.

The first batch of birds had three mortalities. That was superlative. We did the second batch, that was 700. Now we were becoming more comfortable. I went to the farm and spoke with my manager. We agreed to begin selling the birds the following week. I got a call from my manager on my way home that day informing me that the birds were dying. I made research on google to find out the cause and found out that it was heat and stress that was killing them. We tried to salvage the situation. Before we could figure it all out, more than 200 birds had died. That was my first lesson. I also realized that I needed to develop myself by learning more about the technical and business aspects of farming. Google and YouTube were my primary source of learning. I had a big book where I made notes of what I had learned and how I could implement them, my wife calls the book my "Farming Bible."

One day we woke up to the news that the price of poultry feed had moved from 2400 Naira to 3800 Naira. So, I began to make enquiries and found out that the price of corn had doubled. That was when I decided to work with rural farmers to help and support them. This was my journey from self-preservation to personal survival and then to running a business and becoming a social entrepreneur. The journey of working with rural farmers led me to begin to apply for opportunities. Those opportunities led me to win the Young Nigerian professionals forum grant, Tony Elumelu Foundation, Mandela Washington Fellowship, Aspen Fellowship and many other prestigious opportunities and grants.

Aspen Fellowship selects 25 people from across the world. Last year, I was one of the two Nigerians selected. I won the Social Entrepreneurship World Cup to represent Nigeria. To be honest, I recently sat down to reflect on what is next for me. I no longer have any interest in writing grant and fellowship applications. I am now committed to assisting other young stars to grow their businesses. I have evolved, focusing more on crowd funding, offering consultancy services and currently, I work with UNICEF and Red Cross Organization to ensuring food security and safety of vulnerable people.

In summary I will say, overcoming setbacks requires emotional intelligence. It requires a person to step back and reflect on their mistakes and failures. More importantly, it requires a conscious commitment to self-development. In my case, critical reflection made me become aware that I was acting in ways that were inconsistent with my purpose. It made me realize what my purpose was, and the need to hold to purpose. So, when you go through setbacks, ask yourself, am I holding to purpose? What can I learn from my setbacks? In what areas can I further develop myself? These questions can guide your reflection and inspire your comeback.

What you should know about Social Entrepreneurship

Social Entrepreneurship was born out of the problem that Entrepreneurship itself create. Entrepreneurship is purely about capitalism and capitalism is purely about self-preservation. It is purely about profit making. As a capitalist, you don't necessarily care if your staff are dying or customers are dying. All you care about is how much money you are making and that's why you hear of complaints from staff of Big companies like Amazon that they are not being taken care of.

Social Entrepreneurship is a new breed of Entrepreneurship and it tries to break the bond between Not for Profit and for profit. Not for profit and also For Profit organizations have their advantages and they are both good business models. Not for profit only looks at managing social problems for free. This Not for profit model is a grant reliant model. So, someone who runs an NGO is '101 percent' reliant on Grant. Once a grant is finished, his program stops running and they have to wait until the next cycle of grant is opened. Now, you cannot be having social impact and be waiting on doubts, '101 percent'. That is the biggest problem with NGO. The biggest problem with For Profit is that sometimes they go overboard without recourse to the environment or the people or the society or their staff.

Social entrepreneurship is in the middle. It is a business model that allows you to make enough profit to stay in business and to succeed while also being able to do a lot of social good. This should not be confused with CSR- Corporate Social Responsibility. The CSR model is purely for the purpose of advertisement. This typically has no long-term impact. As a social entrepreneur, for instance, I work with rural farmers. I help to increase their productivity and improve their livelihood while doing that, it is a Win-Win for both Me and the farmers. I make money. The farmers make money.

It is not all a bed of roses. It is a lot of work. There are a million challenges you face every day. But as a social entrepreneur, there are things that can keep you going; your passion, resilience, consistency and perseverance, those are things that will keep you going. There is a point where your passion starts to die. For example, if you are not making money, your passion might start to dwindle. Food is to humans what profit is to business and air is to humans what cash flow is to business. Scientists say you will be able to live up to three days without food or water depending on who you listen to but if you don't have air to breathe, you are not likely to live two minutes depending on the capacity of your lungs. Nobody can survive 6 minutes without breathing. A business can survive up to three years without profit and it will be fine as long as it has cash flow. The saturation point is after three years without no profit, it poses serious problems. But if you are able to maintain your cash flow, then you will be able to survive those three years or even more. If you don't have cash flow, you won't be able to survive one day. After the first month, you are already dead.

BRAND COMMUNICATION AND MANAGEMENT

FUAD ABAYOMI SHOBOWALE

Introduction

Brand management is a function of marketing that makes use of strategies and techniques to analyse and plan how the brand is perceived and accepted in the market. The aim of branding is to:

- Clearly convey your brand message.
- Increase the overall perceived value of the brand.
- Capturing your target market for your product or service.
- Generate confidence in the minds of the present and prospective customers.
- Build and raise customer loyalty through positive brand associations.
- Establish an emotional connect with customers.
- Persuade an individual to buy the product.

Importance of Brand Management

The main aim of brand management is to build, measure, and control brand equity – making a brand to have its own value which, when associated with the product, increases its overall value both monetarily and non-monetarily.

In this era of extensive competition where different companies sell almost similar products, a brand is what makes a difference. It helps in positioning the offering in a unique way that provides the company with marketplace advantage and boosts the value of a product.

Creating a brand out of the product not only personifies it, it also creates an experience which stays in the mind of the customers.

Customers recall unique experiences whenever provided with certain triggers related to the product niche or product usage. Creating such an experience around the product not only helps in increasing its sales but it also helps in extending the product line in future.

Summarily, a brand is meant to be visible, unique, different, and better than competitors.

Elements of Brand Management

Brand management includes managing both the intangible and tangible elements of a brand.

Tangible Elements: The product, product price, brand logo, website, social media, packaging, shape, colour.

1. **Logo:** A logo is arguably the most memorable piece of a brand's collateral. Even if someone can't quite recall your brand name, they're likely to remember that visual cue associated with it. A good logo design should be simple, unique, communicative, grab attention, make a good first impression and tell a story about your business ideology.

Some Good Logo Designs with hidden brand messages

Inappropriate Logo Designs

2. **Website:** Your website is the face of your company. While it is true that every public mention or appearance has an impact on your brand, your website is what you are specifically showing to people. Make sure your website is simple to understand and navigate seamlessly from page to page and that the little details like the font and colour palette remain constant. Those design elements, however small they may seem, are an essential part of the brand.

3. **Social Media:** Social media allows you to communicate directly with your audience and establish your brand as trustworthy in their minds, creating an impression that will define how they think or perceive your business. It enables you respond to feedback, answer their questions in real-time, help them resolve an issue, or just check in and let them know that your brand values what they have to say.

4. **Packaging:** Great packaging is especially significant for growing startups because it can have a direct impact on sales and a company's overall appeal.

BEFORE → AFTER

Intangible Elements: Brand Equity, Brand Image, Brand Positioning, Brand Association, Brand Personality, Brand Communication

1. **Brand Equity:** Brand equity refers to the value of a brand and is determined by consumers' perception of the brand. Brand equity can be positive or negative. If consumers think highly of a brand, it has positive brand equity.

Example of Brand Equity.
An example of a brand with high brand equity is Apple. Although Apple or the company's products are very similar in terms of features to other brands, the demand, customer loyalty, and company's price premium are among the highest in the consumer tech industry. Apple ranks consistently as one of the most valuable brands in the world. Apple's brand equity is valued at upwards of US$250 billion.

2. **Brand Image:** Brand image is more than a logo that identifies your business, product or service. Today, it is a mix of the assumptions consumers make based on every interaction they have with your business. It is the set of beliefs, ideas, and impressions that a consumer holds about your brand.

Brand Identity vs. Brand Image
You might hear the terms brand identity and brand image used interchangeably, but there is a difference. In simple terms, you can think of brand identity as what you are saying, and brand image as what people are hearing.

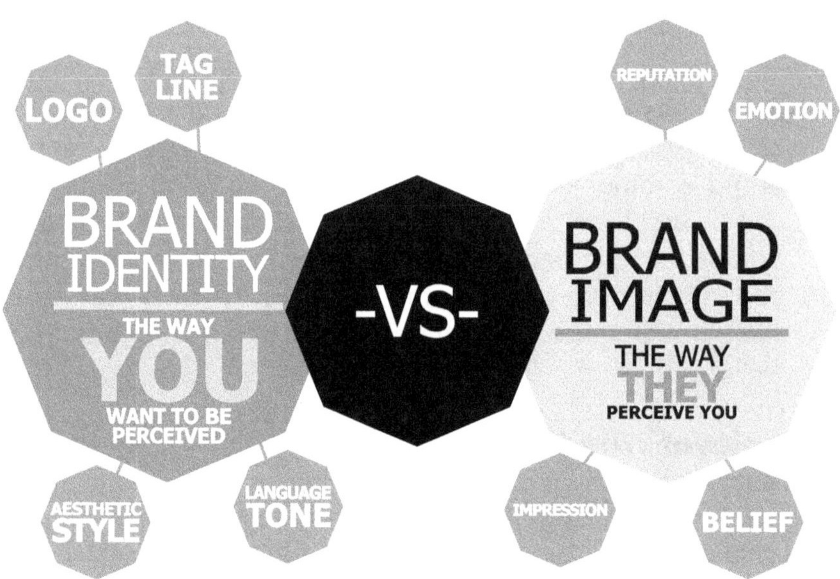

3. **Brand Positioning:** This can be defined as the positioning strategy of the brand with the goal to create a unique impression in the minds of the customers and at the marketplace. Brand Positioning has to be desirable, specific, clear, and distinctive in nature from the rest of the competitors in the market.

    Effective brand positioning enables a firm's brand to be readily distinguishable from competing brands in the marketplace. Distinguishing the brand from other brands can be in terms of associated brand attributes, benefits to users, and/or market segment emphasis, among other factors. Effective brand positioning further emphasizes elements of superiority along one or more distinguishing dimensions, which are valued by consumers.

4. **Brand Association:** This is the mental image formed by the product or brand in the minds of customers due to various brand communications. Brand association is all about how people perceive a brand. When you think about Nike or Adidas, athletic performance and high-quality athletic shoes and clothing are probably the first things to cross your mind even though these two brands manufacture other products as well.

Examples of brand associations are:
- Tesla is electric
- Google is search engine and innovative
- Microsoft is widely used technology (Windows OS)
- Coca-Cola is classic
- BMW is driving luxury and performance
- Apple is simple and innovative marketing strategies
- ZARA is fashionable

5. **Brand Communication:** This is an important tool of brand management by which companies inform, persuade, enlighten, teach, remind, and enrich the knowledge of their stakeholders about the brand, its strengths, values, fundamentals, and its offerings of products and services.

6. **Brand Personality:** This refers to human characteristics associated with a brand. They are expressed as adjectives that convey how you want people to perceive you (e.g. youthful, dependable, energetic, friendly, responsible, sophisticated and so on). It can also refer to demographic characteristics like gender, age, and social class. For example:

- If Harley Davidson were a person, it would be a man. Victoria's Secret, a woman.
- Apple would be a young, hip, creative and Microsoft would be a mature professional.
- Chanel would live in a mansion and TJ Maxx would live in a low-rent apartment.

Brand Personality

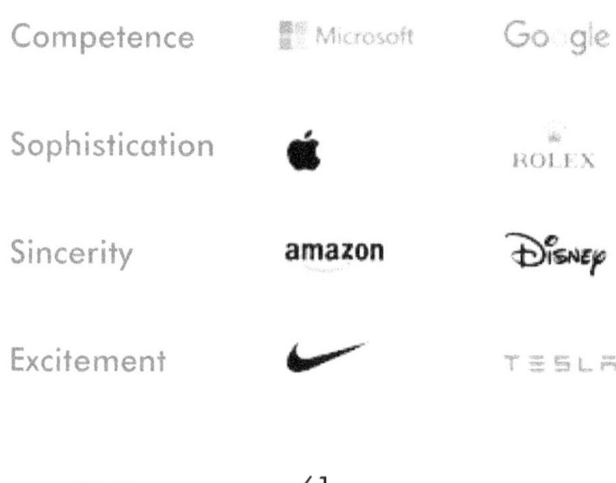

Key Principles of Brand Management
Here are 10 major brand management principles that can usher in business success.

1. **Define your brand and business model**
   A well thought out and defined brand identity should be the backbone of any successful company. Branding encapsulates anything you do that contributes to your customers' opinions and feelings about your company. Brand is how everyone recognizes your business and the first thing everyone judges it by or thinks about it.

2. **Start inside out (Leverage those around you: employees, customers, partners, etc.)**

3. **Connect at the emotional level**
   Develop highly targeted content that appeals to buyers' needs, goals, and interests.

4. **Consistency, consistency, and consistency**
   When creating your own branding, you should strive for that same consistency. Visually, a brand should include the same elements across all channels, such as logo, colour, fonts, message, etc. No matter which channels your customers choose to interact with your brand – your website, your social media platforms, blog, email, or whatever tomorrow's technology may bring – they should all demonstrate the unique experience that your brand represents

5. **Reward Loyalty (Staff, Customers and Brand Ambassadors)**
   Customers should be prioritised, nurtured, protected and incentivised to stay with you. This is where a customer loyalty

scheme can help. The fact is, keeping your existing customers is just as important as finding new ones. Customers should be at the heart of any business. In simple terms, your customers provide your income, so without them you wouldn't have a business. This makes an existing, loyal customer base an enormously valuable asset to your company – and loyal customers spend more.

6. Align your tactics with strategy

Achieving sustainable loyalty, measured in years, requires a strategic sustainable approach. A company must find ways to share value with customers in proportion to the value the customers' loyalty creates for the company. The goal must be to develop a system through which customers are continually educated about the rewards of loyalty and motivated to earn them.

7. Stay flexible and relevant

The market changes every day, and only businesses that learn to adapt and take advantage of those changes can prosper for long. Nearly every industry can provide an example of a prominent and successful business that faded away because it could not evolve, or of a small business that rocketed to success by anticipating changes.

It's crazy to think that 88% of the Fortune 500 firms that existed in 1955 are gone. As the life expectancies of companies continue to shrink, organisations must be more vigilant than ever in remaining innovative and future-proofing their businesses. Below are examples top business that failed because they didn't innovate

8. **Measure brand performance, perception and effectiveness**

9. **Keep competitors closer**

10. **Build a community around your brand**

Brand communication and strategy thinking
A brand communication strategy is a long-term plan for developing a successful brand presence in order to achieve specific goals.

It is a guide that helps transform a company into a brand. It is kind of a light beam that shows you the way and the approach to your audience. It helps you learn how to provide people with additional value in form of high-quality content, and how to communicate with them in a way that will make them love your product.

Brand communication strategy defines who the audience is, what message is to be communicated and what channel is to be used.

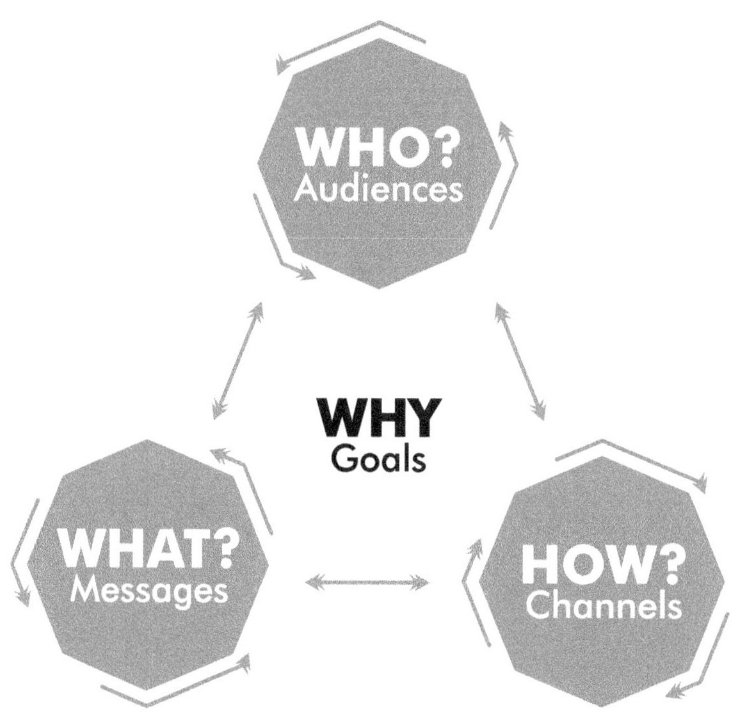

Tools for Brand Communication Strategy

- Offline Brand Communication: Flyers, Posters, TV Commercials, Radio Jingles, etc.
- Online Brand Communication: Website, Social Media (Facebook, Instagram, Twitter, YouTube) etc.

CONCLUSION

A strong brand reduces the perceived safety, monetary, and social risks of the customer to buy a product or service.
When done successfully, brand management can:

- Boost your brand awareness.
- Allow you to charge more for your products or services.
- Influence your audience's purchase decisions.
- Build customer loyalty.
- Increase sales.
- Create happy customers that become brand advocates.

LEGAL EDUCATION FOR STARTUPS (Q & A)

ABISOLA AKINRIN

1. What are the requirements for the registration of start-ups?

Usually, this depends on the type of entity to be incorporated. You could register your start-up as a business name or a limited liability company (Ltd). If you are registering as a Company, you need to provide the following details:

i.   Name (usually you are required to submit two or three names for reservation);
ii. Name(s) of subscribers to the memorandum of association,
iii. Name(s) of first directors (FORM CAC 7);
iv. Complete Declaration of compliance (Form CAC 4);
v.   Statement of Share Capital (Form CAC 2);
vi. Notice of situation of registered address (Form CAC 3);
vii. Memorandum and Articles of Association.

2. How long does it take to register a start-up?

It takes between one to two weeks, where your documentations are complete and free of errors coupled with a functional Corporate Affairs Commission website. However, sometimes your documentations are queried by the Commission upon verification and you will be required to rectify or regularize; and until you satisfy the requirements of the Commission, the process might be stagnant for a while under scrutiny. It is advisable to always get a legal practitioner who is familiar with the process and terrain to assist with the processing of your registration.

3. Does a start-up require the same type of legal obligation like the regular businesses like Limited Liability Company (Ltd) and Public Liability Company (Plc)?

Not exactly. Typically, most start-ups commence operations as Business Names and compliance obligations are not as onerous as Limited Liability Companies. However, as they grow and begin to raise funds for expansion and members grow beyond initial number, it becomes more suitable at that time to register as a Limited Liability Company (Ltd). Once the number exceeds the stipulated maximum number of 50, they are required to get listed or go public as the case may be. At that point they will no longer be referred to as start-ups. Please note that under the new Companies and Allied Matters Act, 2020, the minimum number of persons required to register a private company is one.

4. How can a Founder manage the risk involved in letting others run his business?

Essentially, as your company grows in terms of capital, network, customer base, turnover, goodwill etc., you will need to delegate and focus on business development and branding. At that point you will need to delegate. The bedrock of any successful entity is sound corporate governance. You set the tone from the top. You need the right people who would key into the vision and mission statements of the company.

Most times, shareholders are appointed as board members since they have stakes in the Company. However, in appointing board members, there is need to balance expertise with ownership. You appoint people who possess the technical know-how of the business and people of integrity with clout that can attract business. It is the board with tenets of sound corporate governance that exercises an oversight function over the affairs of the Company. The Board will thereafter nominate a Managing Director that will be responsible for the day-to-day affairs and operations of the Company.

Also, good governance helps your company to attract funding and raise the capital. Angel investors and venture capitalists would insist on good governance before considering your company for investment. At every stage of funding whether bridge seed fund raising, seed fund raising, series A, B C, investors have always insisted on sound governance. You can read the tone from the time you present your pitch deck.

5. **What type of structure can you recommend for a small start-up not buoyant enough to afford a Finance or HR Department?**

For small start-ups, at the infantry stage, the founder is everything. However, it is advisable to get a trusted hand who will oversee the general administration of the Company whilst you focus on the technical and business development aspects of the business. Administrative functions are fused but as you grow you expand your manpower.

SKILLS IN THE GLOBAL SPACE (21ST CENTURY AND COVID-19 FOCUSED)

DIVERSIFYING FOR GLOBAL RELEVANCE

OLATUNJI ADEGBITE

I am almost sure that none of us included the likelihood of the COVID-19 pandemic in our 2020 vision boards. Since Nigeria's first reported case, what started as a denial has graduated to avoidance and now, we are all in panic mode. Virtually everywhere is on lockdown and no one knows how and when this will pan out. COVID-19 has disrupted behaviours and the activities we took for granted.

A question that we may have thought of is, will the world ever remain the same with the way our resilience and humanity have been challenged?

A strong approach to answering this question will be based on how well we diversify for global relevance. Like I hinted earlier, the world has changed and may likely never return to the status quo, what will differentiate those who will win from others are the skills they demonstrate.

These skills can be grouped into two broad sets: Hard and Soft skills.

Hard Skills: These are the skills we typically learn in a formal setting.

Soft Skills: These are the behaviours that may not be easily recognisable in the short term but eventually differentiate talents.

To win in the future, we first have to conduct a SWOT (Strength, Weakness, Opportunity and Threat) analysis of our capabilities and identify our gaps. The next thing is to close these gaps and also align our capabilities to what the global market now prefers.

Key Hard Skills That Will Be More Relevant Post-COVID

- Data analysis and data science: These include coding, machine learning, big data.
- Next are Critical thinking skills, Creativity and Innovation.
- Supply chain and Logistics' knowledge/experience.
- Digital marketing.

Key Soft Skills That Will Be More Relevant Post-COVID

- Emotional intelligence
- Writing
- Presentation and Reporting
- Time management
- Resilience
- Leadership
- Communication

In addition, your ability to display curiosity, how quickly you can learn what you have never known or heard before will differentiate you.

I will advise everyone to read up about COVID-19. This is not the time to spin conspiracy theories. Understand key COVID terms and how they relate to your current work, career and industry. You need to demonstrate that you understand it, know how it will affect your industry, business, company etc and then come up with mitigation plans. Key terms like flattening the curve, cash preservation, business continuity, growth in turbulent times, etc. will be used. It is a race of who can deliver the most with the current challenges.

QUESTION AND ANSWER SESSION

1. **Can you please expatiate on why Data Analysis and Data Science will be more relevant post-COVID-19?**

Response: First, Data analysis is the science of analyzing raw data in order to make conclusions about that information. With COVID-19, a lot of organisations will want to reduce costs and understand their customers better. The use of 21st-century data skills like machine learning, Artificial Intelligence, robots, etc will help them achieve this with fewer humans. Meaning that more things can be done cheaper, faster and easier.

The competition will be hotter so everyone must display some comparative advantage. 21st-century skills are an approach to making life easier for businesses. For instance, I know a company that uses machine learning to prepare and review its contracts in Nigeria. Robots are used by Dangote already and more will be deployed soon.

2. **What is the place of emotional Intelligence Post-COVID-19?**

Response: Because there will be plenty of tension post-COVID-19 due to people losing jobs, family, income and businesses closing down. It will take someone with extra patience and resilience to be able to navigate these tensions adequately. Emotional intelligence is about self-awareness, regulation and then reaching out to others in empathy. Do you now understand why it will be very important?

Guys, you can see why you need to take those lessons on social and emotional Intelligence seriously.

3. How can someone go about project writing? (Business project or the likes)

Response: Key is to understand the industry and context of the project you want to write about. Next is to have solid writing skills. Presentation of the report is also key. I will advise you to use the M-A-C-J approach to writing. You can Google it to know more about it.

4. The whole world is now online. How can a business enterprise or initiative get the attention of their customers seeing that there are now many things getting their attention?

Response: First is to understand the customers. What exactly do they want? Also is to deeply understand what the pain-point/job to be done is. On the soft side, online businesses require a lot of soft skills. Your empathy is key. Educate the customer. Be consistent and patient. Be creative and innovative and deliver all promises. Find your niche and you can grow from there.

5. It appears that science disciplines are at advantage to take on the world ahead. How would you evaluate those in the Humanities (Language

Studies, History, Philosophy etc.) and what suggestions or advice do you have for them?

Response: Good question and you have a point. However, I strongly think that Humanities have a big role to play. For example, Lawyers can be key in Nigeria because we have a largely unstructured environment. Look at Funke Akindele and Falz, Audu Maikori of Chocolate City; they are lawyers and are relatively doing better than others in a shorter time. Above all, we are all human and I will advise that you should not allow the science pressure to get to you. Pursue excellence and success will chase you.

Intermission: On a lighter note, Funke is not a lawyer but a law graduate. For Falz, not everyone will sing, so you can't use them as yardsticks.

What I mean is that a lot of lawyers are using the skills learnt from that course to add value across different industries. We are in an unstructured environment and the ability to read contracts and interpret it very well is a skill most people struggle with. So, the course studied doesn't really matter. What really matters are the skills you can transfer and monetise if that is your area of interest.

6.　I need a Masterclass on LinkedIn. What are your suggestions?

Response: Is it a masterclass you need or you want to improve yourself? There are many ways to skin a cat. So do not fall into the pit of what everyone is doing. Assess yourself, know your gaps and your ambitions and work from there. Perhaps you can expatiate on your question/be specific.

If I may add, avoid putting yourself under too much pressure. Take it one day at a time. We are all learning through these tough times and together we can make it work. Let us all collaborate more.

OPPORTUNITIES IN THE TECH WORLD AND ACHIEVING MORE WITH TECH IN THE COVID-19 ERA

KEHINDE OSENI

Is Tech right for you? What exactly do you need in the tech world? What are employers looking for? What are the opportunities in the tech world and how can these be explored post COVID-19? This presentation highlights some valuable resources to help you acquire some of the highlighted skills.

I am a 2008 graduate of Biochemistry from Olabisi Onabanjo University. Throughout my time at the university, one question lingered on my mind, "…why spend four years for a course whose certificate I might not use?" It was obvious that the resources to get the pre-requisite knowledge to help me forge ahead was very limited. I got worried about this and started to show concern till I got the opportunity to learn Oracle Database in my final year in school. This is a skill I had no prior knowledge of. I took up the training with the hope that it would be a Plan B should I not find something useful with my Biochemistry certificate. This somehow began my career path in I.T.

The compulsory National Youth Service Corps (NYSC) took me to Yola in North-Eastern Nigeria. At that time, the American University of Nigeria (AUN) was in need of a Teacher on Oracle Database. This was an opportunity for me to realize that sometimes we acquire skills for future use as my knowledge in Oracle Database made me fit for the role. In 2015, I was thinking of changing job, to boost my credentials, I obtained a Postgraduate Certificate I.T. This earned me promotions and enabled me work in different capacities as an IT instructor and Assistant Manager in the Training Centre of AUN. In 2016, I left and moved to the United States to be with my family.

The United States presented a different experience entirely. I was looking for different opportunities around I.T, but being a Nigerian and my strong accents made this quest tougher than imagined. I started to explore all other trainings until luck smiled on me and I found one which entailed training people on Salesforce Administration Skills with Salesforce City. A top CRM (Customer Relationship Management system) in the whole of North America with a very huge job market.

Training there involved empowering professionals who have been out of job for a while to learn gap skills, become certified and probably get a job afterward. This was my entry into the salesforce ecosystem. I got a job as the Typist Administrator and I was deployed by Salesforce to a Non-Profit Organization in South California working on issues affecting everyone in South California. I was with the non-profits for a year and few months before I left for another Tech company. To navigate this space, I had to Upskill.

My journey as highlighted above will hopefully help you understand the need to be flexible; to be futuristic; to be willing to learn and gain more skills as you go through life.

Now, ask yourself these questions:
"What do I want to do in the next five years?"
"What are my plans to achieving that"?

To advance to the next level, you need to learn the requisite skills and network with the right people.

Is tech right for you?

To answer the questions posed above, I will say YES. Not because I'm in the tech space but because tech has become an essential element, virtually all fields depend on technology. More than ever, the COVID-19 pandemic has forced more companies to digitally transform or stay out of business.

WHAT ARE EMPLOYERS' NEEDS YOU MUST HAVE?

For those going into the Tech world, Tech Employers are basically looking for two skills. - Technical and Transferable Skills.

Technical skills are hard skills related to the job, graphic design etc. You may not have a background in any of these aspects but the good news is that it is learnable. There is no age limit to learning. It is all about determination, getting the needed resources and support to facilitate the learning process. For instance, I studied Biochemistry while in school and still had to dedicate some time learning Oracle Database, ...anybody can; you too can.

Transferable Skills: A lot of people may be coming from the non-tech background. In spite of their background, they will have acquired some skills that are relevant to the role. For instance, to take up the role of a technical writer role, you probably will need to have had experience writing. This means you should be a very good communicator. This kind of skill will be relevant to tech roles that pay attention to communication skills. You need to know what you can bring to the future world and leverage on that. Acquire skills that will put you ahead of others, skills that will give you an edge. In the true sense of it, most people do not realize they have skills others do not possess. Identify the unique skill you possess and leverage on it.

"You will be the same person in five years as you are today except for the people you meet and the books you read."- Charles Jones. I came across this quote in a book by a Nigerian author, titled *The Habit of Reading is a Gold Mine.* If you take a look at this quote, you would understand that where you will find yourself five years from now will be determined by the books you read, the new things you consciously learn that will serve as inspirations to you or the mentors you have to guide you.

For those going into the Tech space, you will need people with plenty of experiences to guide you along the way. You will need more time learning new things, consciously investing in yourself daily as you traverse. As you go, you may have to deny yourself so many things, spending the bulk of your earning in personal and self-development. You will have to see obstacles as challenges, bearing in mind that with commitments, these investments will pay off sooner than you think. Your career path in the next five years will be determined by the things you have learned and the persons you have connected with.

Opportunities in the tech Space abound in the following:
1.   Social media marketing.
2.   Content marketing.
3.   User experience.
4.   Front end and Back end Development.
5.   Systems and Data management.

We will explore some of these as we move on. You will wonder why social media marketing is Number one. *Crude oil now is people;* your product would be sold to people.   In 2018, Facebook was estimated to have over two billion users and just during this pandemic, some days back, Twitter added a huge number of users on their platform. Today, more people are online because of the pandemic, this means that companies will spend money trying to reach out to people through advert. Now, this part is hot because the skills you need to get the role of social media marketer does not require much spending.

1. Marketing Technologist: The task here involves a person coming up with strategies to market a product or service. First step is to select the technology that will push the strategy out. Required skills here are: project management, writing and oral communication, HTML, CSS, as well as some experience with online marketing. One can also look at the **Social Media Manager** role. Some people out there have soft skills, what they need is the opportunity to deploy such skills effectively. For instance, a platform like twitter is filled with people who are cashing out on the App even though some other persons are there just scrolling through the news and the gossip. The former manages online accounts, from companies to VIPs. A case in point is the former handler of the EFCC twitter account who employed humour in managing the account. He later left EFCC to work in a Bank. Another example would be if AAK mentorship programme decides to have an online presence, they will need someone to manage it to get the information out there. We have many companies because of the pandemic that desire to reach out to people virtually. So, these two roles among other roles are the most sought after out there. To be a social media manager, you have to be familiar with social media platforms like Facebook, Instagram, Twitter, YouTube, Pinterest etc. These are platforms anyone should find easy to navigate; you just need to spend more time learning.

2. Content Marketing: Now more than ever, lots of companies are trying to increase their online presence through their websites, blogs and other digital platforms. From writing, editing, storytelling etc., everyone has transferable skills which can be brought into the tech World. Good writing skills is a pre-requisite for this role. A content manager is the person who ensures the brand of the company and her intended message is passed across through the specific digital platform. A content creator analyses users' engagement to optimize the best platform. There is also the

Content Strategist which is very similar to the content manager but on a wider scope. This entails spending more time researching on how to better engage the audience. The rate of digital transformation at these times makes these roles very lucrative. The skills are becoming more marketable with more people acquiring them.

3.   User Experience: UX and UI: With more organizations including government agencies carving their niche online. The importance of this role cannot but be emphasized especially with the continuous focus on how to improve users experience on their websites and have captivating interface. Opportunities abound with these roles which require a lot of coding skills and can be acquired from online learning.

4.   Front-End Designer and Back-End Developer: The skills required for this role are HTML, CSS, JavaScript and some front-end frameworks. Their major role is to mock up pages to transform them. When you log on to an app, what is happening at the back i.e. behind the scenes is handled by a Back-end developer. Their roles here include Python developer, Full stack, Mobile developer. The front and back-end developers have a common skill set, while the front-end developer does more of coding to make an active website that can be user engaging. The back-end developers are involved and participate in the overall application lifestyle. They provide training, help and support to other team members. Their main focus is on coding and debugging. They collaborate with Front-end developers to define and communicate technical and design requirements. Ultimately, they bring sites to life and make them efficient.

We spend most times accessing the internet on our phones hence we should be more familiar with the Mobile App developer. These

Apps on our phones were designed by mobile developers and they are very common through operating system and MIOS. These skills will be used for apps that will engage the users. Mobile developers are invaluable today because many people engage with their phones and companies wants their apps to be on the phones of people. They develop mobile Apps to enable people access these websites on their mobile phones.

5.   Systems and Data management: We have the Business systems analyst. They are like technology matchmakers. They help customers get profit by leveraging on the systems they have and making efficient use of their tools and drive profitability for such. Many companies are going through digital transformation and they want people to access their site in terms of systems and tools and use that to drive profit. There is also the System Administrator. Typically, this role involves managing software and hardware that the companies have. From computers, to cybers and licenses like Microsoft office. These roles are very easy to get because you do not need a degree and there are a lot of skills involved.

A lot of companies are using cloud base site which makes database roles very broad. This means a person may possess skills for one application but not in others. A data base administrator role in one company might be completely different in another company because of the difference in the technology that each company uses. For instance, a Company might be using Oracle database and a database administrator in such company will spend time working on Oracle platform. Another company might be using Explorer. If you are interested in this role, you will have to be proficient in many databases to fit into roles in different companies. Many companies now have their storage and server online; thus, a **Cloud architect** is needed to help companies make best use of their Cloud services like google drive, Drop Box etc. This role might be useful for those that work in the IT world or wants to go up the ladder. To be fit for this role, there are many skills to learn as it is more of a management role. This means even in the Technology world there is need for people to coordinate the work of all developers in a company. Hence, some of the soft skills needed are Leadership skills, Team Building skills etc. This is a combination of the technical and transferable skills.

Agile Project Manager: Most companies need this in order to ensure efficient management and there are different agile methodologists. There are some skills needed for this role. It is a very interesting role and there are many resources online to help you. You don't need to know how to code but just be able to understand the methodology and good team management skills and problem solving skills.

SPECIALIST GROUP

The role is very specific. **Security Specialist**- Technology comes with its own risk. We have Hackers who can hack into your system. Few days ago, Twitter was hacked. Most of the popular Twitter handles like Barack Obama, Bill gates etc were hacked. They were doing Bitcoin giveaway but Twitter handled the matter. There is also internet fraud. For every company that uses technology, they need someone to protect their system from getting hacked. They want to ensure that there is no data breach. Some companies just want to sell their products and fail to realize that they need Security Expert until their data is breached. If you have detective skills and pay attention to safety, you might want to take up the role of a security specialist. It can be learnt online.

Curious Specialist: When company rolls out softwares, they need people to do the testing. They want to make sure that everything works from end to end. They want to ensure that the tool would deliver all that has been advertised. This also includes hardware. They need people that are meticulous, detail oriented and analytical. Curious specialist are people that are curious about everything and ensure that every detail is accounted for.

This list is not exhaustive. There are more skills but I have to narrow them down. Having all of these at the back of your minds, you might want to pause and reflect on where you belong. You may want to ask "How do I move on from here?" That is why you have this mentorship programme. You have people that are ready to provide you with necessary advice and guide you.

ACHIEVING MORE WITH TECHNOLOGY POST COVID-19

There is a lot to consider. In the past few days, over 400,000 people have been infected with the coronavirus all over the world. The question is, *"When will COVID-19 end?"* I am not a scientist but we might not go back to a normal life in the next two or three years. Even when the virus ends, those guidelines to staying safe will remain. A lot of businesses have gone digital to be able to reach out to their target audience. I overheard someone saying that Tithes will still be paid irrespective of services being held online. What this means is that there is a serious drive to get across to people and this is only achievable through Technology. We need to ask ourselves, *"How we intend to achieve more post COVID-19 through technology"*.

Firstly, there is more opportunity to acquire skills online. Most companies will need people to learn online and will maintain status quo even when COVID-19 ends.

Secondly, people can learn through platforms using applications online. Example; Udemy, Code Academy, App Academy etc. All these provide more opportunities to learn skills online. More resources will be put into these sites. The rates are subsidized because there are so many platforms to learn from. They will provide you incentives and discounts. These opportunities will continue to come up even after COVID-19. More companies will go digital.

As an individual, the first point applies. As a company, the second point applies. You have to embrace technology to survive. If at this stage, you are not using technology to drive your business, you will not be able to compete when the COVID-19 is over. For example, let's look at Education. Many universities are considering distant learning. They will need technology apps like Zoom to achieve their goals. They will need learning management system and people to build and manage these Apps and its contents after it is built. Post COVID-19, there will be more technologically driven jobs.

Thirdly, we would have more opportunities for remote work as companies are moving from physical to online location. This means that you can be in Nigeria and work for companies outside Nigeria. For you to get such remote job roles, you need to be prepared.

Lastly, you can teach technology when you have acquired lot of skills online. This can be used to earn money while helping others acquire the skills you have learned. You can create a website, put your content and earn money by teaching the skills you have acquired during the pandemic.

INTRODUCTION TO GLOBAL CITIZENSHIP

HAMMED KAYODE ALABI

Preamble

When individuals feel their actions affect their neighbours' comfort and other people's comfort across the world, they are referred to as Global Citizens. Global citizenship recognizes that our actions as individuals affect the people around us. Beyond empathy and sympathy, a Global Citizen lives a life of Compassion. Sympathy is where individuals feel sorry for their neighbours' plight while empathy is where individuals understand and share the feelings of their neighbours. However, compassion is where individuals share the feelings of their neighbours and also try to support.

I am Hammed Kayode Alabi - I am here because I am a global citizen and I believe you are too. "You are a global citizen, when you feel that your actions affect your neighbours and other people across the world"

Global citizenship is living in a way that recognizes our world is increasingly interconnected, and that our choices and actions affect other people and communities locally and all around the world.

Who is a Global Citizen? In simple terms, a Global Citizen is someone:

1. Who is aware of the wider community and has a sense of their own role as a world citizen. Someone who makes efforts to

know what is going on both locally and internationally and how these things can make or mar their decisions for a premium life.

2. Who respects and values diversity: someone who understands that people's perspectives might differ from our individual perspectives. A global citizen should value divergent views and develop the skill to accommodate same – socio-cultural intelligence.

3. Who has an understanding of how the world works: someone who seeks to know what goes on around the world, someone who understands that s/he has a very important role to play to make the world a better place.

4. Who is outraged by social injustice: someone who acknowledges the fact that an injustice to one is an injustice to all and does not just show anger towards injustice but make an effort to solve the injustice.

5. Who participates in the community at a range of levels, from the local to the global: someone who attends and contributes in meetings and conferences where decisions on governance and policies that affect his community directly and indirectly are being discussed. Someone who identify global summits and finds access to showcase abilities and roles he or she is playing as a global citizen.

6. Who is willing to act to make the world a more equitable and sustainable place: someone who understands the importance to sustaining current resources to prevent inter-generational

transfer of poverty. Someone whose focus is on sustainability and sustainable development; the development that enables us to meet the needs of the present generation without compromising the needs of the future generation. Sustainable development brings to fore how access to education most times reduces the inter-generation transfer of poverty. Helping others get access to quality education is a good example of taking action towards sustainable development.

7.   Willing to take responsibility for their actions: someone who understands that they are part of the problem and is also committed to solving these problems via collaborations and other communal actions.

Being a Global Citizen means understanding what is going on in your environment and taking actions to ameliorate it. This could be in form of writing and other documentary process about the ills going on in your community to draw attention to these things and effect change. By sharing your thoughts, you are not only contributing to what is going on in your environment, you are also earning your place as a thought leader. The advantage it gives is that it shows you are an authority to be reckoned with. It is one of the key areas to focus i.e. getting involved and showing you are an authority in the knowledge of your environment. To become an impactful global citizen, there is a need to have a good understanding of international politics, and your country's role in the scheme of things. How the policies and laws your country supports affect you in the local realm. For instance, understanding key environmental concepts such as Global South Countries i.e. third world countries - Global North Countries i.e. developed countries and Sustainability Development are steps in becoming a global citizen.

As we set to THRIVE, we need to arm ourselves with societal consciousness and cultural intelligence. A global citizen realizes that I am part of the problem by the actions and inactions – not trading blames. Many times we are tempted to blame the government or the society we have found ourselves in for the challenges we face in life, ignoring the fact that little changes make great differences. Global citizens will switch actions, ask important questions, and get to work – how can I help the government serve my community better? More importantly, as a global citizen, you need to understand that you cannot work alone, an individual needs to collaborate with others, act with courage and compassion.

Global Citizens task: Get a sheet of paper and write 100 acts of global citizenship. From ensuring you take part in volunteer work, community services, to smiling at someone who seems to be having a bad day, to giving a community member especially older/younger citizens a helping hand in executing strenuous jobs. This should contain the responsibilities you want to take for your community in a bid to become a Global Citizen. This does not have to be anything so big, it could be little actions you consciously get yourself engaged in to make your society and ultimately the world a better place.

You should be taking actions of a global citizen today, not tomorrow, not in the future but right now.

SESSION FIVE
LEADERSHIP

THE CHALLENGE OF BECOMING A GREAT LEADER

AHMED ADETOLA-KAZEEM

This discussion is centred largely on insights from the book, "The Nature of Leadership" written by Joseph White.* In the book under review, leaders were divided into two major types, the Mammals and the Reptiles.

The two types of leaders have their good and bad attributes and most of us fall into either one of the types or more tilted to one of them.

Let's consider the characteristics of the Mammalian and the Reptilian leader.

Reptiles
- Detached
- Analytical
- Quantitative
- Independent
- Adversarial
- Focus on Control
- Faith in Evidence
- Rely on Audits
- Value Contracts

Mammals:
- Engaged
- Emotional
- Qualitative
- Interdependent
- Cooperative
- Emphasis on Freedom
- Faith in Others
- Rely on Trust
- Value Community

Which is the better of the two?

Both are vital and most people are a complex mix of the two. We need task-oriented, no-nonsense Reptiles to ensure work gets done and done well. We need people-oriented, nurturing Mammals to maintain the human community through which work gets done. We need both and there's room for both, as long as the Reptiles meet a threshold of civility and the Mammals produce good work. There are, of course, problem reptiles (selfish and destructive) and problem Mammals (slackers and gossips). Organisations falter, fail or don't reach their potential both because of leadership that is inadequately Reptilian and because of leadership that is inadequately Mammalian.

Reptilian Excellence: Leaders need to be tough and tough-minded at times, thick-skinned and even cold-blooded.

Why do leaders need to be tough?

1. Toughness gives their organisations a chance to survive.

2. Toughness sets the tone at the top.

3. Toughness establishes and maintains authority and credibility.

4. Toughness gets things done.

5. Toughness ensures strong management which is just as important as inspired leadership.

Being a tough leader means:

1. Paying attention all the time to the big picture and the details, to the clients and customers and your people, spotting needs and risks, problems and opportunities, achievements and failures, making sure they're addressed, handled, and recognised.

2. Making economically sensible decisions and being on top of numbers.

3. Having a plan and seeing to its disciplined execution.

4. Measuring performance, including your own, on results, not intentions.

5. Exercising strong, competent management of resources and ensuring effective control.

6. Saying "No" when required and saying it directly, clearly, firmly and unambiguously.

Leaders must display exceptional toughness in six areas:

1. Understanding financial matters.

2. Setting the bar high and making sure it doesn't slip.

3. Dealing with bullies.

4. Serving as judge and jury.

5. Cutting costs, staff, budgets, facilities, etc.

6. Litigation

Mammalian Excellence: Leadership excellence cannot be achieved through toughness alone, that is why there is a need to combine toughness with the nurturing spirit of the Mammals to ensure that organisations thrive.

What it means to be a nurturing leader:

Achieving Mammalian Excellence requires three leadership attitudes and practices:

1. Treat people with dignity and respect.

2. See and develop the potential in people.

3. Make it about your people, not about you.

Capabilities to achieve Mammalian Excellence:

Certain dimensions of strong Mammal leadership are personality-based and rooted in early childhood development. There are, however, things aspiring leaders should know and work on that will make them far more effective on the people side of the leadership equation. Some of them are:

1. **The Dream Deal:** Smart leaders do two things exceptionally well in recruiting and motivating people. They understand people's dreams and show them how joining up and performing at a high level will enable them to achieve those dreams. And they sell the organisation's purpose and culture as a means of achieving dreams people either have or might want to consider adopting.

2. The Leadership Triad: Stretch, Support, Connect
What most organisations and most people need most of the time are new challenges to embrace, perspective, breathing room, someone to believe in them, and resources and tools to meet the challenges they've decided to take on. In other words, they need stretch-support-connect from their leaders.

3. Be an effective communicator and a good listener

4. Remember that a good idea can come from anywhere and from anybody.

5. Maintain a sense of humour.

Becoming A Great Leader

Because of our biases and experiences, we are naturally bound to tilt either towards the Mammalian or Reptilian leadership style and sometimes view the other leadership style with aversion. However, a great leader combines both styles for the following reasons:

1. Leaders must be Reptilian because organisations are challenged to survive in a competitive, Darwinian environment and because they are populated by fallible human beings who are, at times, negligent, fraudulent, ornery and bullying.

2. Leaders must be Mammalian because organisations are composed of human beings who are free to choose the organisations with which they affiliate (it helps leaders to think of employees as volunteers), possess the knowledge and ideas

the organisation needs to thrive, are capable of amazing and wonderful things, and are hungry for inspiration, challenge, achievement and recognition.

3. Leaders must be Reptilian because people need order, stability, routines, and resources in order to perform productively, reliably and efficiently.

4. Leaders must be Mammalian because people need attention, room to grow, and someone to believe in them in order to do their best, learn and be creative.

5. Leaders must be Reptilian in order to establish authority and exercise power. They must be Mammalian because people deserve to be treated with dignity and respect.

6. Leaders must be Reptilian to stand up to harsh and threatening competitive environments. They must be Mammalian to embrace and empathize with suffering humanity.

7. Leaders must Reptilian because organisations need good management. They must be Mammalian because people deserve good leadership.

8. Reptilian leadership improves the odds that an organisation will survive. Mammalian leadership improves the odds that an organisation will thrive.

Ultimately, we must all strive to be great leaders who effectively combine the attributes of the Mammals and the Reptiles and even more.

Qualities of Great Leaders

Let me share with five qualities of great leaders:

1. Being innovative- They are innovative and don't succumb to conventional wisdom.

2. Being an intelligent risk-taker- They take calculated but significant risks that pay off.

3. Having an appetite for top talent- They surround themselves with extraordinarily talented people and bring out the best in them.

4. Developing the "helicopter view"- They have an unusual sense of perspective, looking ahead, back and sideways.

5. Exhibiting the "sparkle factor"– They have good personal qualities- presence, charisma, magnetism - that make them "sparkle".

Leaders come in all shapes, sizes and types. Some are reptiles, the cold-blooded, tough-as-nails decision-makers with their eyes on numbers and a focus on control. Others are the mammals, the warm-blooded, compassionate creatures who connect with those around them and build success through trust and open communication.

Good leaders combine the best attributes of both. And the truly great leader is the one who transcends type and moves beyond usual barometers of success to achieve real change in his or her organisation.

*B. Joseph White, *The Nature of Leadership*, Newyork: AMACOM, 2007

CLIMBING THE CORPORATE LADDER

NOJEEM SUBOMI YUSUF

As introduced, I would be guiding and providing tips on how I believe we could all be successful in the corporate world. I am going to be pulling largely from my experience, having worked in the corporate environment for the past 9 years. In those years, I have also interacted with many other corporate workplaces being a consultant that manages several other corporate clients. While I take us through, I would provide practical examples as much as possible. I would emphasize areas that are universally correct and also mention where I think are applicable in a few environments.

Tip 1 - Have clarity about your career goals.

Being clear about your career goals, in my view, means you are clear on what you expect the peak of your career to look like.

As a fresh guy from school, your definition of your career goals can be quite broad, but as you grow in your career, you begin to streamline and make it a lot more specific. For example, when I started out, I wanted a job that allows me to use my analytical strength and my love for numbers to positively impact the businesses of those that I choose to work in.

Somehow, my first job was with KPMG as a tax consultant, even though I studied Agriculture. But it was in line with my career goals because it involved working with numbers a lot and being analytical - which perfectly fits into my broad career aspirations.

As I grew, I began to redefine my career goals - and now, I have defined the peak of my career as when I attain a tax leadership role in a multinational environment where I am identified as one of the global thought leaders in taxation.

So, you should also attempt to define your career goal irrespective of the stage of your career. You could take a pen, spend the next few minutes to identify what your genuine career goals are, without being beclouded by peer pressure, undefined love for money and fame, and careers in vogue.

Tip 2 - Identify career options and workplaces that are likely to help you achieve your career goals.

When I started out, my understanding then was that the best places I fit in were in investment banking/consulting environments and private equity firms. So, I focused my attention on them when I was searching for my first job. Along the line I came across a KPMG advert, even though I really didn't know what they did, I made my findings and then realised their objects kind of aligned with my aspirations, so I applied and the rest they say is history.

You may not be as lucky as I was, which is why I recommend going through a subsidiary list of workplaces if your desired workplaces are not welcoming you. Later in your career, you can always switch over. Research thoroughly before you apply to any work environment. When I say research, I would emphasise that you find a way of talking to someone who works in the kind of work environment you are applying to. That kind of person is more suited than anyone else to provide you with job application guidelines.

I recommend you talk to at least two qualified guides before you apply and while you go through any recruitment process so you can get enough information. I always do this.

Tip 3-Be competent at your job.

You would need to speak with a competent professional in your discipline to help you properly define what it means to be competent.

Tip 4- Possess sterling communication abilities.

Speak and write good English without errors. Never come up with the excuse that English isn't your mother tongue - you probably learnt English for at least 18 years, so it is never going to be acceptable in most places.

Tip 5- Be street smart.

Up until now, I have talked about introductory tips. Going forward, I would focus on tips on how to do well in a corporate environment.

Tip 6- Understand what it means to be a top performer.

Be a top performer as defined by your employer and your immediate boss. When you are in a sane corporate workplace, performance is key and you need to be clear on what top performance is. Have a session with your boss and anyone else that may be involved in your performance appraisal to be clear on what you need to do. Document this.

Tip 7- Do a good job and keep evidence.

It is not enough to do a good job. It is a lot more important to document the great stuff you have done.

It is a fact - superiors easily remember the bad things you may have done and easily forget the good things you do. This is why you need to document to help them remember when it is time for an appraisal.

All sane corporate workplaces have a system for documenting employee performance.

Tip 8 - Check in with your superiors and obtain feedback frequently.

There is a tendency for you to believe you are doing a good job, but remember, you are not the one to conclude your performance appraisal - so it is important you regularly check in with your boss to understand how well you are doing and get corrections on things you need to fix.

When you do this well, your boss is unlikely to document your weaknesses during appraisals - because those check-ins suggest you are committed to being better.

Tip 9 - Open up when you make a mistake.

When you make a mistake, particularly a costly one, don't attempt to cover it up. Please engage your boss, explain how it happened and propose remedial actions. Even when you get a bad hit, your boss will be clear that there is nothing else hidden. She can always trust you to open up when you are struggling with your job

Tip 10 - Never try to be smarter than your boss.

If you are an extremely smart person, you should not be tempted to prove you are smarter than your superior, particularly in the presence of others. Almost everyone that has done this, lives to regret it.

There may be a few cases where it is the right thing to do and can fast-track your career growth. Only the most skilful about office politics try this.

Tip 11 - Be socially enlightened - don't just know your job and nothing else.

It is important you understand how your job contributes to the success of your employer. You should not just do your job because you have to earn your pay, without understanding the extended impacts of what you do. Understand the business of your employer, general business and political environment. Socialize as much as it does not infringe on your principles. Make friends with colleagues and your bosses if they are willing to. Do not force yourself on anyone.

Tip 12 – Do not be an ass licker.

An ass licker deceptively wants to always look good in the presence of the boss, sometimes at the expense of others. A smart boss will notice this and will mess you up when the time comes.

I would give a personal example, in one of my previous jobs, I was probably the only team member that was not very close to our boss. I do my work, say hi when we see, wish him well when he celebrates and that's about it. Others will typically flock to his house frequently to visit, but I was still rated better than them.

Tip 13 - Be receptive to feedback.

Do not be unnecessarily defensive, admit your errors – do not be too defensive when your boss gives you feedback. Challenge your boss' view when it's critical - don't always agree. If you spot any critical mistake on your boss' part, please mention to him privately - don't do it too often and never do it in the presence of others.

Tip 14 - When you have a bad boss, you may ultimately have to leave that workplace.

This is how to know a bad boss. One who gives you undeserved promotions. One who never corrects your mistakes - he picks the job from you and does it himself- that is a very bad boss.

You are unlikely to grow with someone like that. For that kind of boss, you need to demand feedback and regular check-ins. You need to help him to help you, otherwise, you may be rendered incompetent and useless. The other extreme is someone who hates that you are successful - but you have to be careful because this is tougher to identify. This may just be a strict person - so you need to discuss with your mentor to analyse whether or not you really have a bad boss.

Tip 15 - When you have to exit your workplace, exit well.

Never leave on a bad note - even if the employer is the one exiting you. Resolve any disputes you may have. Get feedback from as many of your superiors as you can. Keep in touch.

I'll give a practical example. When I left one of my previous employment, I had an unresolved conflict. It lingered even after I left, but I had to resolve it with the person involved. Guess what, in one of my subsequent job searches, the would-be employer was a very close friend of my former boss that I had an issue with. The would-be employer relied solely on the positive feedback he got from my personal boss that I previously had an issue with. Yes, I didn't take the job, because something more relevant showed up, but what if I didn't have a choice and I also didn't resolve my conflict? What would have happened in the end?

You always need a mentor to do well in a corporate workplace and you need God too.

QUESTION AND ANSWER SESSION

1. Can you please expatiate on how you were able to navigate your career from being a graduate of Agric to being a Tax specialist that could function exceptionally in a multinational space. Did you simply focus on professional courses while studying Agric in school?

Response: While in school, I focused on my Agric courses - no professional exams. But because I was then interested in investment consulting as a career. I was always reading about it and following business news. That made me very aware of finance and investments - that's probably what stood out for me at the KPMG Interviews. I started taking professional courses like ICAN when I got my first job.

2. As an entrepreneur, how does this impact us? I have never worked in a corporate organisation.

Response: My comments are largely applicable to persons who have bosses within an employment relationship. You are a boss in what you do and probably an employer of labour. My tips today are at best, good for your awareness. I am not sure it is very relevant for you.

3. **If you work in the public sector, one you are very clear is not a sane environment. You need to leave, how best do you do it? You work in a public secondary school and so many things are wrong with the setup, the pay is not so good but regular. You have been there for about 7 years and it is difficult to pursue a PhD in such an environment, you want to leave for a higher level but thinking about finance. Lecturing in a higher institution is your goal. How best do you go about it?**

Response: First thing, never blame the environment for any condition you are in. Even though there may be reasons to do so. But if you keep blaming your environment, you are unlikely to find a way out.

Yes, the pay is usually poor in public secondary schools, and teaching in a university is not the only alternative. As you have said, you require a PhD to be a university lecturer, which you presently cannot afford. I know there are good-paying teaching jobs in top private schools. That may be an option for you. You need to find out what you need to get those jobs. Please don't be one of those that believe you need to know someone influential to get those jobs – it is totally false.

When you get such good jobs that help you to save money to do your PhD, you can then find your lecturing job.

4. **You said we should allow our bosses to appraise us. Do we need to do our self-appraisal before or after we get feedback from our boss?**

Response: Yes, you need to do your self-appraisal, which was why I said document evidence of the good things that you do. I also said you should check-in with your boss and obtain regular feedback. All these are part of self-assessment.

5. **How do you become disciplined in order to follow a planned work schedule to achieve set goals?**

Response: I was guilty of this for so many years. I now use the stick and carrot approach for myself. I give myself a reward if I follow my plan diligently and deny myself of certain rights if I fail to. You may consider it if this works for you.

6. **From Agriculture to Tax Consultancy, how did you achieve this feat in KPMG using an Agriculture degree? Can you kindly explain to me what exactly constitutes a corporate environment? For some of us that are still struggling with getting placements that align with our career goals even after graduation, what would you suggest?**

Response: KPMG wasn't really looking for Accounting graduates. So, I really didn't do anything special. Of the 42 of us that joined KPMG tax that year, only four studied Accounting, and more than 4 of us studied Agriculture. There were even more guys that studied engineering courses. You may need to broaden your career goals, you can't afford to restrict it to what you studied at school. If you don't mind, we can have a private session together to discuss this at length. They wanted smart and young people irrespective of their background. Which is why I recommend you understand the requirements of any job you are applying for before you start the process.

7.   How do you handle hostile co-workers who see you as a rival while climbing your career ladder or a boss who sees you as a threat because of your capacity? Also, how were you able to build resilience in order to improve your stress threshold so you could work under pressure in the corporate world?

Response: People like that are everywhere. Ignore them and continue to do a good job. Be friendly as you can with them, and treat them well. The corporate work environment is not necessarily stressful. Some places are, others are not. I don't enjoy working under pressure, so I may not be the best person to recommend how to improve your stress tolerance level.

8.   What happens when you work under a very weak boss that can't defend himself not to talk of defending his subordinates? All top managers know he would accept anything they throw at him. Is it not better to be smarter than him?

Response: Remember I said in a few cases, it may be wiser to prove you are smarter than your boss. This is one of those cases, but it can be very delicate to do. You need to be clear that leadership works in your favour, and that your boss doesn't have sympathisers in leadership.

9. **How soon can one retrace steps if one has lost clarity on career goals considering age? What are the likely challenges one could face when trying to change career to suit the desired goals?**

Response: It's never too late to redefine career goals. My dad worked with the civil service for about 10 years before he moved to the private sector - his peers at work were 10/15 years younger than him. His boss was 5 years younger than him.

There's likely to be a skill gap which leads to the pressure to deliver, and the inability to cope in a different kind of work environment.

You need to get your family to understand your career goals. Also, keep them in mind when deciding your goals, you can't just expect them to allow you to focus on your career without considering them. Your family is a key stakeholder in your career.

10. **What advice can you give to someone who seems smarter than the boss, and has a good performance record both within and outside the work environment but the boss will always hijack his thought, present and execute his idea?**

Response: You may need to find subtle ways of letting the bosses of your boss know that you are the engine in your boss' empty head. It is pretty tough to do. If you have mentors in that same workplace who you trust and can keep whatever you tell them secret, have a conversation with such people. You will likely get more relevant action points.

11. If one is older than average intake age, is there any way one can still get into top corporate space? What would you advise those working in a low-level one-man business environment where promotion targets are seemingly very rare?

Response: The reality is that today's corporate world discriminates against people who are generally older than persons at the same competence level with them. However, there are a few places that don't discriminate, so you need to find those places and focus on them. You may also need to rapidly upscale your competence and knowledge base. Identify a mentor in your chosen profession to discuss this with.

ABOUT THE CONTRIBUTORS

Ahmed Adetola-Kazeem is a Lawyer, Arbitrator and Coach. He is the Managing Partner at Adetola-Kazeem Legal Practice. He is a member of Board of Trustees of Lagos Public Interest Law Partnership (LPILP) and the Chairman, Board of Trustees of Network of Pro Bono Lawyers. He is also a member of the Board of Trustees the United States Exchange Alumni Association and many others. He founded Q-MADI Taekwondo Club, a multiple award-winning club, nurturing street children into world-class champions. Three members of the Club represented Nigeria at the African Games 2019 in Morocco. The Club has also produced a Commonwealth Gold Medallist and many National Champions at all levels. He recently conceptualized AAK Human Capital Development Centre, to inspire the next generation of leaders across different human endeavours. He is a 2017 Mandela Washington Fellow and Presidential Precinct Fellow; He won the 40 under 40 Legal Rising Star Award in 2019 and was a finalist at the International Bar Association Pro Bono Awards 2013 in Boston USA, among several numerous awards and recognition. He conceptualized and edited this book.

Mr. Disu Kamor is a dynamic professional engineer and manager with vast cognate experience in the construction, publishing, oil and gas industry in Nigeria, UK and Ireland, spanning over 20 years. He graduated as the best HND student in the department of Agricultural Engineering of the Kwara State Polytechnic in 1992 and subsequently completed his BEng study in Mechanical Engineering at the University of Port Harcourt, Rivers state. He has both professional and post-graduate qualifications in Engineering and Corporate Finance and Administration in Nigeria and UK. He had worked with NLNG Limited, Shell Exploration and Production, Ireland, Shell Exploration & Production, UK, ERKAM Publishing Limited, Turkey and Holoflex Limited, a smart metering company. Currently, he is a Director at ZGM Investment Group of

Companies Limited as well as the Executive Chairman of Muslim Public Affairs Centre, MPAC. Disu is a professional member of the Irish Society of Petroleum Engineers with executive roles in a number of charity and humanitarian organisations. He has also won many recognition and awards in both his professional and social careers.

Kabiru Olanrewaju is a first-class graduate of Accounting from Obafemi Awolowo University, Ile-Ife. He is a member of the Institute of Chartered Accountants of Nigeria (ICAN), the Chartered Institute of Taxation of Nigeria (CITN), and the Chartered Institute of Management Accountants, UK. Kabiru is a finance professional with several years' work experience providing financial management solutions to local and international clients, including government MDAs. He is working with a team to help small businesses create governance structures that make successful businesses outlive their owners and individuals to achieve financial freedom.

Abisola Akinrin is a vibrant, hardworking and dynamic Attorney. She is Senior Associate at Tope Adebayo LLP's Corporate/Commercial and Secretarial department and she has been at the forefront of a couple of landmark commercial transactions. Her experiences span different sectors including Legal, Educational, Insurance, Information Technology and Banking in different capacities and at different times. She has extensive experience in capital market, corporate governance, legal and regulatory compliance, company secretarial practice, legal audit and due diligence, corporate financing, corporate restructuring, divestments and investments, asset recovery, and estate administration.

Usman Ali Lawan is the founder and CEO of USAIFA International Limited, a sustainable farming venture that practices and promotes zero waste agriculture. Under his leadership, USAIFA is using farming to solve the dual problems of hunger and unemployment. Lawan also founded "Farmer-In-Suit" (www.farmerinsuit.com) – an online Agric investment platform which crowdsource funding from professionals and use it to provide micro credit, farm input and extension services to smallholder farmers. He also partners with the Dangote Business School at Bayero University, Kano, Nigeria to provide master class training in Agribusiness Development, starting and sustaining SME in Africa, Funding Opportunities for SME, Business Plan Writing and Developing Business Strategies for SME. Lawan is a regular speaker on TV, Government & Universities fora and the TEDx. He is an Aspen New Voices Fellow, a Tony Elumelu Entrepreneur and a recipient of the Mandela Washington Fellowship for Young African Leaders.

Nojeem Subomi Yusuf is a tax expert who is currently a tax services manager with Deloitte, the world's largest professional services firm, by all metrics. Nojeem provides professional tax support to the largest Nigerian businesses, privately incorporated and publicly listed on the Nigeria Stock Exchange. He provides tax advice to US and EMEA parented companies with presence in Nigeria. Over the last 9 years, Nojeem has built a tax expertise in the following areas: corporate tax compliance, tax controversy management, tax accounting & reporting, local & international tax advisory, tax support on corporate reorganisation and M&A transactions, tax risk management, tax function set-up and efficiency assessment, and a bit more. Nojeem had previously worked with two other Big 4 firms, KPMG and Pwc, at earlier stages of his career. At some point, he joined Dangote Group as an Assistant Tax Manager, and later rose to become the Group Tax Manager of its Flour Group. He is an associate member of the Institute of Chartered Accountants of Nigeria.

Onyedikachi Ekwerike is an A-list mental health practitioner, leading change in the mental health space for the past 7 years. He is the founder of Postpartum Support Network (PSN) Africa, an organization aimed at raising awareness and supporting women struggling with perinatal mood and anxiety disorders in Africa. Onyedikachi is a first-class graduate of psychology from Lagos State University and holds a master degree in clinical psychology from the University of Lagos. He is a 2017 Mandela Washington Fellow, and a 2018 Global Leaders Fellow. He is currently a doctoral candidate at Kansas State University.

Kehinde Oseni is an Enterprise Systems Administrator adept at using Salesforce.com platform and other cloud-based technologies to optimize business processes and proffer business solutions. He started his career as an Oracle Database instructor at the IT Training Centre at the American University of Nigeria (AUN) where he rose to the position of Assistant Manager. In his seven years at the AUN, Kehinde led the IT training program for both internal and external clients. He also provided critical database support directly to stakeholders on multiple complex projects. In 2015, Kehinde was honoured with the Most Outstanding Staff award for his department at AUN. In 2016, he moved to the United States and is currently a Senior Salesforce Administrator at PagerDuty - a cloud-based incident management platform. In 2019 He was honoured with the JVS Employee of the year award. Kehinde strongly believes in giving back and spends his leisure time mentoring upcoming Salesforce enthusiasts. He is currently looking to extend his Mentorship skills to Nigeria.

Hammed Kayode Alabi is a Social Entrepreneur, Author, SDGs Youth Champion and Educator with 12 years of experience in active citizenship and volunteering. He is currently the Fellow-in-Residence and Regional Manager at Peace First, a global non-profit in the United States. Hammed currently leads its core programs in Sub-Saharan Africa and supports youth-led movements in Nigeria, Kenya, Malawi, Zimbabwe, Madagascar, and others. He is also the Founding Executive Director for Kayode Alabi Leadership and Career Initiative (KLCI), where he has supported over 3232 students in underserved communities in Nigeria to develop life and 21st century skills needed for the workforce and future of work.

Shobowale Fuad Abayomi is a graduate of Computer Science from the University of Benin, with several years of professional experience in Media and ICT Services and Consultancy; Brand Communication and Management; ICT Management, Operation and ICT Project Execution. Fuad in his professional career has worked with the Nigerian Television Authority; Airtel Nigeria; and ASO Television Abuja (FCT owned TV station). Fuad is the founder and co-manager of Vericop Technologies and Integrated Services, a start-up business outfit in Abuja with services and business interest that encompasses Innovative ICT Business Solutions; Branding, Prints, Video Production, Animation and general media services; Digital and Social Media Promotion and Marketing; Cloud Computing Services; Web and Mobile App Development, Administration, and Maintenance; Data Analytics, Warehousing, Security, Recovery and Restore; and Agribusiness.

Olatunji Adegbite has over 12 years' experience in strategy, supply chain management, transformation, financial advisory, management consulting, due diligence, and auditing across multiple industries and SMEs in multicultural environments. His skills and competencies include but not limited to strategy, competitive intelligence, transformation, capital/projects contracting, pre- and post-award contract management, supplier management, project management, formulation and execution of category, sourcing and negotiation strategies, materials management, business planning, integrity, financial & commercial due diligence. He has worked for several Fortune 500 companies and he is the founder of Naspire, a social learning, and market intelligence platform helping professionals and entrepreneurs in Africa succeed. He writes African Business Stories that provide relatable contexts to global concepts thereby accelerating learning and understanding.

THRIVE

THRIVE is an encompassing 'manual' for your growth in the various stages of achieving your dreams in life. It is a compendium of presentations by highly successful professionals.

Are you looking for a book to serve as a training manual for corporate staff, social entrepreneurs, tech enthusiasts, management staff or soft skills development generally? Are you a youth struggling with finding your career path? Wondering what's the next stage in accessing opportunities to fulfilling your dreams? Confused about managing a profitable business yet making social impact? Or totally clueless about dealing with people and building potential connections?

What if you can get answers to all your questions from one source, a book that identifies your problems and proffers intellectual and practical solutions, highlighting the step by step approach to a successful career and business, with emphasis on the core values of resilience, recovery and growth.

It is a must read for everyone out there to learn, unlearn and relearn.

Edited by

AHMED ADETOLA-KAZEEM

ISBN: 978-978-984-160-8